Black, Gay, Britis

Black, Gay, British, Christian, Queer

The Church and the Famine of Grace

J. A. Robinson-Brown

scm press

© Jarel Robinson-Brown 2021

Published in 2021 by SCM Press
Editorial office
3rd Floor, Invicta House,
108–114 Golden Lane,
London EC1Y 0TG, UK
www.scmpress.co.uk
SCM Press is an imprint of Hymns Ancient & Modern Ltd
(a registered charity)

H
Y Ancient
M
N &Modern
S

Hymns Ancient & Modern® is a registered trademark of
Hymns Ancient & Modern Ltd
13A Hellesdon Park Road, Norwich,
Norfolk NR6 5DR, UK

Scripture quotations are from New Revised Standard Version Bible:
Anglicized Edition, copyright © 1989, 1995 National Council of the
Churches of Christ in the United States of America. Used by permission.
All rights reserved worldwide.

The second verse of the hymn text 'When Jesus came to Jordan' (Fred Pratt
Green, 1903–2000), © 1980 Stainer & Bell Ltd, 23 Gruneisen Road, London
N3 1LS, www.stainer.co.uk, is used by permission. All rights reserved.

Marty Haugen, 'Let us build a house where love can dwell', *Singing the Faith*,
London: The Methodist Church, 1994, © GIA Publications, is used by
permission. All rights reserved.

The prayer from Holy Communion Order One from *Common Worship:
Services and Prayers for the Church of England* is © the Archbishops'
Council 2005. Used by permission. rights@hymnsam.co.uk.

British Library Cataloguing in Publication data

A catalogue record for this book is available
from the British Library

978-0-334-06048-2

Typeset by Regent Typesetting

Contents

To the memory of my Uncle George aka 'U.G.'
~ George Antonio O'Brian Robinson ~
1952–2020

'Venite ad me omnes qui laboratis, et onerati estis,
et ego reficiam vos.'
Matthew 11.28

One writes out of one thing only – one's own experience. Everything depends on how relentlessly one forces from this experience the last drop, sweet or bitter, it can possibly give. This is the only real concern of the artist, to recreate out of the disorder of life ...

James Baldwin, *Notes of a Native Son* (Penguin, 2017)

Foreword

by Professor Pamela Lightsey

There is a lot to be said about matters of loyalty and covenant in many professions of our time. Here in America, we often hear about the blue line. This is a strong culture of solidarity among police officers that supports even the criminals within its ranks. Silence is not demanded, it is assumed. It is a rare event for police officers to turn against their peers in order for justice to prevail. Clergy also work under specific unspoken rules of solidarity among peers even though it may be to the detriment of parishioners. At its lowest moments, the hierarchy of the Church has gone so far as to codify the harm it is willing to commit against human beings despite the hypocrisy and immorality of their stated agenda. One has but to look through the annals of Church polity to see the directives and theologies against Africans, Native Americans, women and now the LGBTQ community. People have been slaughtered, enslaved and communities pillaged as a result of those directives and theologies.

Rather than remain silent about the oppression of Black Queer Christians in Britain, the Revd Jarel Robinson-Brown has taken the matter of his ministry seriously by speaking truth, even when it is uncomfortable and even dangerous. Of this current work he writes,

> It is a book that speaks of the grace of God as God's special and unconditional love for all people, and of how that grace is not offered as it should be to Black LGBTQ+ people in the Church of God. It is also a book that unapologetically centres Black people as both the subject and the audience although it seeks to challenge Christians of all backgrounds who are neither anti-racist nor LGBTQ+ affirming.[1]

What Robinson-Brown has given us is a work unfettered by the politics of the Church or the myth of whiteness.[2] He has dared write about racism within the Church and how that racism harms Black British persons. The argument that he presents about the Body of Christ in Britain – that the predominant whiteness in Christian spaces and the famine of grace in the Church – is part of a rich continuum of liberation theology that demands the Church live into that divine Word which it says is the source of its very being.

To be sure, anti-Black racism is horrible and worthy of interrogation, yet utilizing an intersectional approach, Robinson-Brown goes deeper. That is to say, the Black lives that he lifts up are those of Black LGBTQ+ Christians. The trauma and suffering that they have experienced contradicts the gospel preached from many pulpits. Too often it is at the hands of the Black community. Even that homophobia coming from Black people is influenced by anti-Blackness. It emerges from a people who are wrestling with internalized oppression and the ways whiteness remains the bar, indeed the goal, for the 'better' human being.

Like many before him, Robinson-Brown highlights how the Christian community has demonstrably failed Black people, and particularly Black LGBTQ+ Christians, rather than give into this unacceptable standard. It should come as no surprise that his approach to the sacred text, the Bible, journeys through the historical use of scriptures to enslave Black people. The wretchedness, if you will, of the then Negro as perceived by those who enslaved them: their perceived brutishness. This twenty-first-century author, Robinson-Brown, wrestles with this notion of wretchedness as given in the lyrics of 'Amazing Grace' and from the ontological perspective of a Black queer man. Rather than embrace the stereotypes of our existential condition, Robinson-Brown refuses to cede Blackness or queerness to the machinations of white supremacist culture no matter that such culture comes draped in ecclesial garments. Or, shall I say, precisely because such culture comes draped in the garbs of the Church universal?

Instead, Robinson-Brown guides the reader through a fascinating approach to one of the basic tenets of Christian faith, the saving grace of God. This grace is without limit and, for Robinson-Brown, it is that gift of God that does not require Black LGBTQ+ Christians to make choices about their very being. 'Grace for LGBTQ+ people is only really grace when it reaches into our love, our blackness, and same-sex desire with gentleness, affirmation and love.'[3] One is gay and Black, gay and Christian , gay and Jamaican without any concern about the capacity of God to love and to extend saving grace without the oft demands to choose, to give up, to betray one's self as only living a 'lifestyle' rather than simply living as one made in the image of God.

The Incarnation, God made flesh among us through the birth of Jesus Christ, is the loving work of God in order to offer an unlimited and underserved love to humanity. That work, according to the author, does not surrender even to the inevitable brutality of the cross. Indeed, it is this Christ on the cross that is ultimately rendered, a queer body.[4] This grotesque image – rebuked, mocked, scorned and torn – reveals God's ultimate love for humanity. It is a love beyond the powers of that time and remains beyond the power of today's hetero-normativity and white supremacy.

As an aside, it seems to me that one would certainly be right to question the violence of the cross and the terror that it symbolizes as a resource for Black LGBTQ+ liberation. Must the way to liberation be paved by martyrdom? It is an ongoing debate. If we are to debate, then we must hold in tension what the author has well-articulated: the purpose of the birth of Jesus Christ. God came even knowing what was ahead.

As a Black American queer lesbian womanist scholar, I was profoundly delighted to read the history of Black LGBTQ+ British people. Perhaps I should thank the author for the hours that I will spend learning more of persons like Justin Fashanu, Patrick Nelson, Ivor Gustavus Cummings OBE, Pearl Alcock, Rotimi Fani-Kayode and Berto Pasuka. He has done a great service by whetting our research appetite. If we join with what Robinson-Brown is venturing upon, I imagine not only our two countries but persons in other countries – where Black LGBTQ+ persons struggle to see themselves centered in the conversation for justice – will benefit.

As it stands, in *Black, Gay, British, Christian, Queer*, Revd
Jarel Robinson-Brown has lifted his voice. Rather than submit
to the silencing demanded not only by overt racists but also by
so-called 'good liberal' white LGBTQ+ persons – Christians
and those who claim no faith. He troubles the waters of
whiteness within the LGBTQ+ community. My experience has
taught me that this is *the* troubling that is most revealing in
the queer context. Daring to confront racism and homophobia
are all fine and good within the LGBTQ+ community. One can
even depend upon a good number of 'allies' doing that sort of
work. However, it becomes an entirely different matter when
Black people confront racism within the ranks of the LGBTQ+
community. It is then that one becomes cast as recalcitrant
and, in the case of white LGBTQ+ Christians, any safety net
as a minority within a minority is suddenly in jeopardy. No
doubt this knowledge is behind Robinson-Brown's assessment
regarding the needs of the Church:

> It needs the true and living God, not the god of the White
> Supremacist imagination, but the foot-washing, crucified,
> wounded God revealed in the Black Jesus who did not cling
> to power or earthly glory, but who empowered the down-
> trodden and persecuted.[5]

It is this subtle interplay between Black liberation theology and
Black Queer theology that gives his final chapter, indeed this
book, its most captivating element. Robinson-Brown brings it
all together in service to the eradication of a kind of putrid
ideology that is as dangerous as the pandemic that has nearly
brought humanity to heel but for the fantastic scientists working around the clock. He argues for a work among scholars
and theologians 'to make the sun-kissed Jewish Jesus visible'.[6]
Still, in the Church as with the pandemic one always finds the
staunch resisters who refuse to believe fat meat is indeed greasy.
They do tend to make you want to throw up your hands and
exclaim, 'I'm tired of this church!'[7]

Rather than whole-heartedly reject the Church – which has
little clue about its Black LGBTQ+ membership – he advo-
cates for a Church of Jesus Christ that offers salvific and

loving grace to all people and does not confer sin upon Black LGBTQ+ persons solely based on their gender identity, orientation and to whom they give mutual consent to share love. Moreover, any church that is not willing to welcome Black LGBTQ+ persons but instead, through its polity, hierarchy, missives and sermons, harms them is a church, an institutional body, that must be abolished. In truth, I have for quite some time taken the position that the institutional Church must die if it refuses to comport itself to the message of Jesus Christ. It is that Church, the body of Christ, that shall never die.

What do we Christians do with this gospel message, which beckons with words that project an image of the Beloved Community, which requires the 'casting down' of everything that exalts itself above the true and generous grace of God? I read Revd Robinson-Brown suggesting we enter the work with humility then make assiduous efforts to stand in God's all-inclusive love and to welcome others into that love. This is an unflinching, compelling indictment of Black LGBTQ+ oppression within the walls of the Church. At the same time, it is a poignant, impeccably written narrative that offers us invaluable insight that will help a famished body receive the grace to feed its soul and be transformed.

The Revd Professor Pamela Lightsey, PhD
Meadville Lombard Theological School, Chicago

Notes

1 Jarel Robinson-Brown, *Black, Gay, British, Christian, Queer: The Church and the Famine of Grace*, London: SCM Press, 2021, p. xiii.
2 See James Baldwin, 'On Being "White" ... And Other Lies', *Essence Magazine*, 1984.
3 Robinson-Brown, *Black, Gay, British, Christian, Queer*, p. 31.
4 Ibid, p. 72–3.
5 Ibid, p. 156.
6 Ibid, p. 164.
7 Ibid, p. 152.

Preface and Acknowledgements

As I started to write this book, the entire world began to change. The fragility of our human institutions and systems suddenly became as visible as their deadly potency. As our bodies became separated through physical distancing, and human touch restrained by lockdowns and isolation, we found ourselves facing an unseen killer. In the midst of this, the world we knew swiftly became unrecognizable, one in which we were told where to stand, how long to wash our hands for, and to cover the parts of our faces that we have retrospectively discovered communicate so much. We have experienced the very real double-edged sword of the necessity of touch, and the abuse of touch evidenced in rising cases of domestic violence, LGBTQ+ hate crimes, and multiple incidents of racist violence. This pandemic, or rather our response to it, has governed our intimacies, interrupted our spiritual life, and managed our funeral rites and by extension our grief. In the UK it has silenced our singing, closed our churches, and rendered visible our societal sicknesses and inequalities at a time when Black LGBTQ+ youth have been hit hardest.[1]

Writing this book, about Black Christian LGBTQ+ lives, at a time when the vulnerability of all Black life has unavoidably shaped the tenor of my writing, has made a difficult task much more challenging. Not only has the absence of library access been a hindrance, but I have had to let go of how I imagined the entire process of writing. Between the higher rates of fatality among us throughout this pandemic, as well as the killing of Ahmaud Arbery and Breonna Taylor and the very public and brutal murder of our brother George Floyd in Minneapolis, I have tried to press on with a task that has, in light of this, felt even more urgent. Not just that, but this is a world in which race is now being discussed in a way in which, when I began writing in 2019, it simply wasn't being discussed in the UK. The emotional toll of bearing witness to Black LGBTQ+ Christian faith, and trying to hear the voice of God in the midst of a writing task that has required the study of deeply tragic stories and our traumatic history, has meant that the shape of this book has been determined by this experience. I say this to say that this is not perhaps the book I expected to write, but the book that these circumstances have given birth to. It is a book that speaks of the grace of God as God's special and unconditional love for all people, and of how that grace is not offered as it should be to Black LGBTQ+ people in the Church of God. It is also a book that unapologetically centres Black people as both the subject and the audience, although it seeks to challenge Christians of all backgrounds who are neither anti-racist nor LGBTQ+ affirming.

For the first time in 800 years, churches in the UK have had to close their doors during this pandemic. In this period, I have heard Christians from backgrounds of wealth and privilege express their sadness and longing at the Church 'turning its back' on them, shutting the door 'just when we need the Church most', expressing a sense of betrayal. I've also heard of Christians expressing how they 'miss Holy Communion', really 'miss hymn singing', and 'miss the fellowship we normally have'. Some have unequivocally told me that it is now more than ever that the Church ought to be 'standing with the fearful and vulnerable'. These multifarious articulations of sacramental hunger and embodied Christian community are things many privileged and heterosexual Christians are experiencing for the very first time. But I cannot help but notice that Black LGBTQ+ Christians have known this hunger and lived with it for years – that we who are Black and LGBTQ+ live constantly in a state of emergency. We know what it is to lose our spiritual home, be turned away from the Church's sacraments, and have the doors shut in our faces. We know what it is to lose the sense of spiritual 'family', to lose the safety and assurance that comes from being able to worship God in the way we once knew, to have routine and normality disrupted and to suddenly feel isolated – we know. And in our exile from our families and from our spiritual homes, we have, in so many cases, not been sought out … but been left in a wilderness where grace is in famine, and where love and welcome, sacraments and singing are scarce. Those who are experiencing this for the first time because of the pandemic should count themselves blessed that their 'exile' is due to a virus and not their identity.

When I first agreed to write this, I was determined to do one thing: write a book that did something to help set Black Queer Christians in Britain free. If I have achieved that, if I have in one way or the other pushed back against the violent religious, particularly 'Christian', forces that make it difficult for us to breathe in this life, in this world, in this Church – then I will rest in that knowledge alone. There are many more books that need to be written, and I want to encourage those of all faiths and none who are Black and LGBTQ+ to write, to tell their story, and to speak (if they feel safe enough) about God from their perspective and experience. Perhaps we never feel safe enough to tell the truth from where we stand? You must decide what 'safe enough' looks like for you! There are, of course, Black Christians who are not from my Christian tradition, and I am aware that many Black British Christians will be from the Charismatic, Pentecostal, Oriental Orthodox or Independent Churches – my own experience of Christianity as a British-Born Jamaican includes many of those, but I write primarily as one shaped and committed to a High Wesleyan Sacramentalist/ Afro-Catholic tradition within the Anglican Church.

Finally, no work like this is completed without the help of friends and supporters. The idea for this book originated with a paper I gave on Grace and Black Queer Bodies at Warwick University during the Society for the Study of Theology Conference in 2019. The encouragement of colleagues at that conference, who have become allies and friends, was crucial in the genesis of this book. Outside of that group there are others who have been instrumental in the writing of this. I'd like particularly to thank my oldest friend – my beautiful older sister, M.R.B. – who inspired me to read and write as a child, and from whom I learnt so much in the earliest part of our childhood about the importance of education. In a fundamental way, nothing I have ever written would have been possible without her. I am, in everything, eternally grateful to my chosen family

... my 'ride-or-dies'. I can never thank Mel, my 'Ufan mi', enough for being the best best-friend and soulmate, and Tom for being the best embodiment of a straight White Christian ally. To Kamari and Dwayne for challenging my originally limited ideas of God and gender and for being an image of faithful Black Queer love. To Sekai Makoni for her friendship, honesty and wisdom – you constantly inspire me. I should thank my Black Queer elders: Fr Jide Macaulay 'Moma Jide', Ajamu X, Lady Phyll Opoku-Gyimah, Marc Thompson and Dr Rob Berkeley – you are beacons to me, and a witness to the possibility of survival in this world. There are those too who encourage me without even knowing it, in particular my friend and mentor Anthony Reddie aka 'Prof', Dan Yomi, my 'padi mi', and Moses, Dr Kesewa John, Florence O, Josh M, Selina S, Suwit 'pom dee peun', Grace Pengelly and Alina Jabbari. The beautiful folk at the Black activist KIN network: Kennedy, Zahra and Ayeisha – being part of KIN's first convening truly changed my life. Thanks too to Fr Robert Thompson and Carles Garcia Jane for their hospitality and love, particularly this year – and for the loan of books in this pandemic. I'm extremely grateful to David Shervington for his encouragement and support as Senior Commissioning Editor throughout the entirety of this process, without whom this work would not have been possible. Lastly, I want to thank the beautiful people of the Parish of Putney, St Mary's and All Saints, and my colleagues at King's College London – places that have been life-giving springs in the famine, and have shown me unconditional welcome and love.

This is, really, like all my work, part of a long love letter to Black folk.

I love you, I love us ... and so does our Ancient God.

J. R. B
The Feast of St Sebastian
London 2021

Note

1 www.pinknews.co.uk/2021/02/22/black-lgbt-youth-covid-19-mental-health-just-like-us/, accessed 1.3.21.

one day,

it will all make sense.

And the myriad of

moods we say
'Good Morning' to will be one

One day.

The sun will shine,

and curtains blow
with the pure winds of freedom
that we are yet to know.

They will come.

Rushing in, like the tears,
and the sorrow, and the hues we know so well
but cannot name.

one day we will write
in the past tense
about the present as we
dwell
in

the future.

one day, we will laugh
till we cry. miss the last train. together.
one day, we will be

Old, and black, and gay ...

one day we will have made it ...

... and 'it' will all make sense.

J. R. B.

Introduction

Am I loved? Do I have worth? Is my life worth living? These three questions are things that no human being should have to truly contemplate. Worse still to be driven to ask themselves, indeed the world, while simultaneously entertaining the very real possibility of the answer being 'no'. Yet these are three questions that I have in my own life asked myself, pondered, wrestled with, and largely, in fact entirely, because of my position in the world as someone who is Black Queer and Christian. I suppose in part, much of what I think renders a book like this necessary is the fact that when I and those like me have asked these questions, the Christian community, and our own African/Caribbean culture as well as all that surrounds it, has regularly failed to help us answer them in the affirmative if we have dared to utter our truth. Rather, we have been left wondering, or in some cases wrestled with these questions for so long and in the absence of an answer that we have indeed decided that life is not worth living, and chosen to do something about that. To say this is to bring home the reality that telling Black Queer folk that they are of value and loved by God is radical, life-saving and urgent work in a racist, transphobic and homophobic world such as this. This clear statement of God's love for all people has, for me, been a central part of my priestly vocation in both the Church and the world. In simple terms, that is what this book seeks to do from within a Christian framework where grace is given primacy.

I write as someone whose identity crosses many of society's boundaries, in that my experience and my personhood feel inherently intersectional. I am a Black Queer British Christian minister of Jamaican and Cuban heritage.[1] I am, therefore, not a disinterested observer of issues related to human sexuality in either the Church or the world. I am passionate about the equality, freedom and justice due to those who are lesbian, gay, bisexual, transgender, non-binary, intersex and queer, and I long for the day when our erasure and queer-antagonism ceases and our lives in all their diversity are allowed to thrive within and without the Church. The gut-wrenching reality of course is that this is not yet the case. There is what I have termed a 'famine of grace' in the Church today. By this I mean that the Christian community as it currently exists is living in a time in which the grace of God for all God's beloved children feels as though it is in scarce supply. To listen to the stories of Black LGBTQ+ Christians in the Church is to learn the harsh truth, which is that love is lacking for Black Queer Christians in the Body of Christ, and this lack of love, symptomatic of a lack of wisdom, is nothing other than sin. When famine descends upon a land the result is that people die, of hunger, of thirst, of starvation – they are deprived of life and all that relates to it. God's beautiful Black Queer Christian children are sacred yet dying of a spiritual hunger and starvation they have been thrust into, and the Church of Jesus Christ today finds itself so utterly obsessed by gender and sex that it is fail-ing to notice the effects of its behaviour. For most Black Queer Christians the discussions around same-sex marriage equality in the Church feel futile when questions of racial justice and Black LGBTQ+ inclusion fail to be honestly addressed. While Black LGBTQ+ Christians search for sources to feed their spiritual hunger beyond the Church community, the Church seems to be degrading and denouncing anyone whose lives are not straightforwardly heterosexual. Yet, at the same time, con-fusingly the Church of Jesus Christ also invests much of her time proclaiming that God's love is 'for all' and that 'all are welcome', while simultaneously practising a form of drip-down grace-onomics, dividing God's children between those who can immediately bask in the joy of God's love and those who must change and transform beyond all recognition before the love of God can *truly* be theirs. We are divided as the 'deserving' and the 'undeserving', the 'pure' and the 'impure', the 'good' and the 'bad', the 'well behaved' and the 'naughty', the 'saint' and the 'sinner', both frequently and shamelessly. Where Jesus intended unity, the Church has established binaries that it now cannot live without but only some can live within. The Church of Jesus Christ today lives upon the propagation of a deep heresy that proclaims (when truly examined) a theology not of salvation by trust in Jesus Christ, but rather of 'salvation by faith, work and heteronormativity'. As thousands upon thousands hunger for the gospel of redemption, grace and love, the Church has found itself more invested in the exertion of power over people's bodies while the cupboards of the Queer poor remain empty, and young Black children become estranged from both family and communities who refuse to accept them because of 'what the Bible says'. In this, many Black and White Christians find a common unity in their hatred of LGBTQ+ life. Those who suffer most from this troubling reality are those whose voices, experiences and bodies the Church has chosen to ignore, silence and destroy – and to demand silence from those whose truths you are not yet ready to hear, when they have less power, is nothing other than an act of violence.

When this violence has been done to us, as Black Queer Christians, we are prone to the spiritualization of our suffering. We wonder if this is perhaps part of the cost of our freedom – God's judgement upon us for what we have been told to believe is our sin, or the painful growth needed to become our better selves. Some carry the pain of this violence with them for their entire lives and afford it no name or reason; others who 'survive' this violence nurse their wounds beyond the walls of the Church, finding another faith or belief system in which to seek community. Some seek and never find, while still others walk away from religion altogether. Still others find this act of violence so severe that having wondered (and wandered!) for so long if they are loved by God and their family, they heartbreakingly end their lives prematurely. Bad theology is deadly, and bad theology in a time when grace is in famine is deadlier … Black and White cis-heterosexual Christians are not the custodians of Christianity, and they are certainly not the sole inheritors of God's grace. Grace is the quality of God's love for us. Although this is something on which all Christians agree, there has been no consistent usage of the word 'grace' by all Christians. It has both a substantive and adjectival use and

3

cannot be understood unless it is experienced. This means that for those whom the Church treats as being beyond God's grace, the Church itself is distancing people from experiencing it. Our language of grace can inhibit our experience of it, and this can have the deepest consequences for LGBTQ+ spiritual lives. To experience grace we must be in touch not only with our own lives, as they are, but with the life of God as God's life is. The experience of grace is fundamentally a human experience of the divine love of God. Without personal human beings experiencing in their Christian lives the grace of God, there can be no Christian doctrine in which grace appears. This means that Christian communities in which Black LGBTQ+ people, and all that we are, are desired is fundamental to our experiencing of God's grace within the Church. As the Jesuit theologian Roger Haight has said: 'It is in the saint that one has, as it were, a concrete and actual manifestation of grace, and it is grace for the world.'[2] There can be, therefore, no experience of grace for all in a church in which radical inclusion and God's love for all people is not at the centre. It is this that makes Christian communities truly Christian, and this alone that enables all of us, no matter who we are, to experience the God whose very love is grace.

The Church understands itself in both its theology and its behaviour to be the Body of Christ, but it seldom seeks to ask why the Body of Christ in so many places and situations appears to be lacking the open and visible presence of Black Queer bodies in its congregations and its leadership – if indeed Black folk are present at all. Nor does it consider why it appears to have baptized, confirmed and consecrated Whiteness as the embodiment of a true Christian and pious civility as true holiness. No one seems to ask the question: where are the visible, beautifully Queer Black people of God within the Body of Christ in Britain, and who is feeding their spiritual hunger? I believe a major reason for the invisibility of folk like myself in the Church is the behaviour of the Christian community in which there is evidently this famine of grace. To pretend that this 'famine' was the first in the Church's life would be to ignore its 2,000-year-long history. Actually, Christian communities, the Body of Christ, the Church, have always been at their core a group of people struggling to work out who and what they are for, who and how God can love, and what sense (if any) grace makes in the life of the world. Even in the very beginnings of the Church, among the early Christians we witness a church using its power far too often to exert control over God's children in the same way the Empire exerted its power over the body of that innocent Brown body, Jesus Christ. Yet, despite it being so evidently clear and evidenced in the life of Jesus Christ that our primary task in all things is one of love, mutual service and mercy, we still seem to get it painfully wrong. Whether we view the actions of the Church in relation to how it has navigated its way through the abolition of the slave trade, the ministry of women, the inclusion of LGBTQ+ individuals, or the place of divorcees within the Church, what we witness time and again is a church that places far too little emphasis on the theology of grace as the unbounded goodness and love of God. Its victims? The very people of God for whom Christ gave his life. It would be comforting to think that we are on the path to progress in relation to the intersection of race and sexuality. But even those who in recent times have written from a Black Christian perspective regarding race and the Church have failed to consider the lives of Queer Black people. Again we experience erasure, as heteronormative faith in the dialogue around race is perpetuated as the norm. Ben Lindsay, in his very necessary challenge to the 'UK Church', made some startling observations about the lack of Black people within White denominations, but sadly no consideration was given to Black church leaders like myself or others who feel doubly excluded within White-majority British Churches.[3] Any liberation theology that claims to be Black theology must take seriously the voices of all the marginalized and oppressed, including that of the LGBTQ+ community. I fear that Black Queer Christians in Britain will fail to be included in the conversations around both race and human relationships in the Church if we do not begin our own dialogue and confront the teaching, structures and systems of the Christian community, of which we deserve fully to belong, with the truth that is written in our experience. As the Black theologian Professor Anthony Reddie so powerfully said in 2012:

> Over the years I have come to the firm belief that one's commitment to the full inclusion of LGBTQ people, whether conceptually or in more activist terms, represents the litmus test for one's authentic praxis as an advocate of Black liberation theology.[4]

This test is one that many Black Church leaders in Britain have failed to pass, often through an illiterate or overly simplistic reading of scripture combined with a focus on the holiness that is supposedly wedded to heterosexuality and heteronormativity. It is these leaders who, although they may appear committed to Black liberation, are not committed to liberation for all people and who, hiding behind theological convictions and heteropatriarchy, suggest that anything other than heterosexuality is not just sinful but inherently 'un-African'. Many of these church leaders, through their dehumanization of Black LGBTQ+ lives, forget that the very idea of 'the self to which sexuality attaches is itself an artefact of the colonial encounter'.[5] As Black Christians the work we need to do to free ourselves from a colonial reading of Christian theology, holy scripture, Christian history, as well as our own and other bodies, is monumental. By the time we come out of the closet many of us have become Queer theologians, historians and biblical scholars out of necessity – for our own survival. No one, it seems, ever truly ponders just how conducive sexless Christianity is to those of us coming from communities where our bodies are regularly shunned and eluded. The Church becomes a safe haven, then, for those who are fundamentally anti-body, anti-desire and anti-sex ... for those who are nurtured in a Christianity which can only lead to low self-esteem, and which is guilt-ridden and harmful.

Scripture in particular has played a huge and largely detrimental role in the Black LGBTQ+ experience. In every house I lived in growing up, there were always many books, but always central to everything there was a Bible. Open, laid out, positioned; usually on its own little side table in the living room. The *living* room did what it said on the tin, it really was the place where as a family we ate, argued, laughed and cried together and apart. Constantly open, the Bible reminded us that we belonged to a story, that the 'Word of God' was part of our narrative, that we were not just any people, but we were Christians. I remember as a child finding it strange that something of so much apparent value was allowed to remain there, gathering dust mostly, hardly ever handled or read or turned beyond Psalm 23 left open to protect us from evil and harm … from the world. Somewhere between the Good Shepherd who 'maketh me to lie down in green pastures and leadeth me beside the still waters' was White Jesus whose eternal threat was embroidered into some random gift from Jamaica which told us, or reminded us, that 'Christ is the Head of this House, the unseen Guest at every meal, the silent listener to every conversation'. In other words, Jesus is 'Massa', watching your every move, listening to every desire and longing, one who is unseen but always seeing, silent but always listening … a kind of God-freak. This rendered Jesus less of a 'Good Shepherd' and more of a threat. It presented the Word of God as something that read us, rather than us being able to read it. Many years down the line I now have a better relationship with scripture, and have found my place within its pages. But there was a time when, like so many Black LGBTQ+ people, I came across some of its words that made me question the very deepest truths on which I once stood, or in which I at least trusted and took for granted.

It isn't easy for Black folk to get away from the Bible. I have been amazed at times how inherently connected our lives as Black people seem to be not just with God but with the Bible. In so many ways – in our music, our storytelling, our cultures, our history and the legacies that have shaped us and the nations we are connected to – the words of the Bible are all-pervasive. How often have we heard, from people who are Black but have never entered the doors of the Church or blown the dust off their Bibles, 'Look, at the end of the day the Bible says it's wrong!' 'It' being 'us' … the ways we love, feel, have sex, dress, walk, identify, carry ourselves … the shape of our desire, our longings, our names and friendship groups. Matthew Vines, in his book *God and the Gay Christian: The Biblical Case in Support of Same-Sex Relationships*, deals beautifully with the 'clobber passages' of the Bible so often used against the

LGBTQ+ community. *Black, Gay, British, Christian, Queer* is written on the explicit understanding that there is no biblical or doctrinal foundation for the exclusion of LGBTQ+ people within the Church, and Matthew Vine's work is essential for those who might like to understand why I am so firm in that conviction.

The use of the Bible against LGBTQ+ people makes it very hard for any of us to believe that we have a place in God's family, and even harder for us to hear the truths that scripture seeks to speak to us. The violent use of the Bible against women, Black folk and the LGBTQ+ community does not make it clear that 'Christianity is about a message of radical, boundary-destroying love. Christianity rightly understood is about the transgression of boundaries. Christians believe in a God whose love undoes every binary'.[6] To write a book like this might give the impression that one text can contain the whole breadth of Black Queer Christian experience. It obviously can't. There will be many stories that go untold and the truths of which this book simply cannot reflect. My hope, however, is that there will be a kernel of truth here to which every reader, whatever their background, might be able to relate. I hope it is the start of a new conversation, or the continuing of one. I am intentionally in this book seeking to avoid what might be considered formally as a 'Black Queer Christian Theology' in the academic sense, akin to other Queer theologies, but I am thinking theologically about Black Queer life. I believe such work serves a noble and necessary purpose, but my aim in this book is to affirm, celebrate, encourage and love those who are yet to discover Queer theology at all. I suppose also this book is an attempt to avoid the erasure of our faithful and faith-filled lives. I fear that without this type of work people of faith like myself, who often find ourselves absent from the 'mainstream' of anything, will continue to go unnoticed. What some do not consider is that part of the privilege of being White is that life does not demand that you think about it. Even in the LGBTQ+ communities White Queer folk are alleviated of ever considering how race and sexuality interplay. We, who are marginalized as Black and LGBTQ+ within mainstream denominations and within wider British culture, need White Christians in Britain (who find themselves not only in the majority but often in leadership even in Black-majority congregations) to grow not just in empathy (which requires the intelligence of love) but more crucially, in courage. I am convinced on one level that it is the accumulation of so many past lies about our life together as Christians and about the people the Church has demonized that is at the heart of our present trouble, and not one of us really wants to hear or tell the truth. In the task of truth-telling, I have been helped by those who have told the Church the truth from the foundations of their love for it. James Cone, a Black American liberation theologian, asked in his seminal work *God of the Oppressed* two questions, which I find myself wrestling with deeply today, and which we should all ponder:

> When does the Church cease to be the Church of Jesus Christ?
> When do the Church's actions deny the faith that it verbalizes?

Cone proceeds to say:

> For the sake of the mission of the Church in the world, we must continually ask, What actions deny the Truth disclosed in Jesus Christ? Where should the line be drawn? Can the Church of Jesus Christ be racist and Christian at the same time? Can the Church of Jesus Christ be politically, socially, and economically identified with the structures of oppression and also be a servant of Christ? Can the Church of Jesus Christ fail to make the liberation of the poor the centre of its message and work, and still remain faithful to its Lord?[7]

We might also ask: can the Church neglect the primacy of grace in its dealings with and relations to God's LGBTQ+ children and *still* be the Church? What I propose here is very simply a renewal of our commitment as God's people to the fundamental reality of grace for *all* as something that permeates not just our language but our behaviour, and even our definitions of inclusion, equality and diversity. I am not interested in a church or a gospel that offers the love of God with a page full of terms and conditions. Either all people are made in God's image or they are not. Either Christ came, died and rose again for all or for none. Either the Church exists for every soul or for not a single soul. It is time the Church made up its mind about what God's posture towards God's people truly is. It is time the Church made up its mind about how far the love of God can reach, because the ambivalence in our current life is costing precious lives, many of them Black and Queer. It's time for the Church to be the Church.

Grace of course is messy, because love is messy. In many ways, this messiness informs my motivation in my choice of terms. As someone who identifies as gay but is actually more accurately described as bisexual, I have found that the Church in its wish to control my body and desire has repeatedly failed to hear my expression of bisexuality in the past and seen me as someone who, along with other bisexuals, has the potential for heterosexuality. Indeed there have been official documents in the Church of England for example that have suggested that it would be preferable for someone identifying as bisexual to choose heterosexuality, and enter 'heterophile relationships' leading either to celibacy, abstinence or heterosexual marriage, as if such a choice were possible.[8] Queer as a term sets me free, both from this violence and also because it is a truer reflection of the sense of freedom I claim as a child of God who need not define myself simply for the sake of being understood by another. Depending on the context, I use 'Queer', 'gay' or 'bisexual' and retain the right and freedom to do so. The cultural norms within which we exist can be powerful tools of oppression, forcing us to enter into binaries that, while pleasing to others, lead us more deeply into falsehoods which when established must be sustained and when erected always fail to set us free. Further to this, as a Black man I have found the term 'gay' and even 'bisexual' too often to be reminiscent of the dominant White-male image of the LGBTQ+ community, which so often portrays a racially exclusive image of the Queer community. I hope that readers will understand my motivations behind the choice of terms, a choice that I intend to be inclusive of the varied and diverse LGBTQ+ community, and realize that part of what I understand about the love of

God is the freedom for us to express ourselves in terms of our identity with liberty and confidence. Those who love, understand from the heart.

I have found in so many spaces that Black LGBTQ+ people in Britain who are of a similar age to me and from a similar background are much more comfortable with the term 'Queer' than those who came before us, for whom it had a totally pejorative character. In various spaces I have encountered Black Queer folk, and even on social media 'UK Black Queers' is a familiar-sounding description of many spaces. My use of certain terms in this book, and even the occasional use of patois, indicates, I hope, who I believe to be my primary audience.

So, why am I writing this book? I'm writing it because I have a vision of a different kind of Christian community, one which I suggest is unable to contain the Church, institutionally, as it currently is. I'm writing it because I have found so little in the context of the United Kingdom that engages theologically with people like myself. I write it because I wonder what the Christian faith, as embodied by the Church, would look like if we seriously lived according to our belief that Jesus *really* did die for *all* people? What would our conversations around sexuality (in those places in which we are having them) look and feel and sound like if we started from the point of grace rather than the point of mercy, with its implication of someone somewhere having fallen short? What if we spoke about God without always naming the explicit sinner who so often happens to be a person just like me: Black/Brown and LGBTQ+? Is it possible for us as Christians to have a dialogue about human sexuality without entrenching our discourse in the language of sin, salvation and repentance?

This book seeks to say to the Church and the world, boldly and with love, that Black Queer Christian lives matter. It seeks to remind the Church of those who find themselves beyond its fellowship, absent from its priorities, out of its sight, thrown out of the fold, yet who directly suffer from the perpetual ecclesial terrorism of the Christian community through its speech and its silence. I want to name and acknowledge something of the pain of Black LGBTQ+ Christians and to speak to hearts and souls who know what this intersectional identity feels like.

Lastly, I want other Black Queer Christians to realize that the gospel is our story as much as anyone else's, that the Church is our home despite what it may feel like, and that Jesus Christ our sibling, Saviour and friend is alongside us, came into this world for us, and walks with us as we seek to find our home in his body – the Church. Beginning with the idea of grace as communicated in song and Christian community, the earliest chapter explores the challenge that occurs when our personal story collides with the Church's reality and our taking it at its word. We move then into a theological exploration of what Christ's birth means for the world, and particularly LGBTQ+ lives, and what his death means to our Queer bodies and flesh, and particularly to human suffering. In this I explore the lives of other Black LGBTQ+ people, particularly in Britain, and how their stories of LGBTQ+ trauma and the language of the Christian community are not disconnected. The closing chapter seeks to offer an ultimatum to a Body of Christ that is resistant to change and which returns to the themes of grace and repentance not as the goal for the LGBTQ+ Christian, as is all too familiar, but for a sinful and fallen Church.

Notes

1 I write about a portion of my own experience as someone who is ordained and living at the intersection of race and sexuality in Ruth Hunt (ed.),*The Book of Queer Prophets: 24 Writers on Sexuality and Religion*, London: William Collins, 2020, pp. 98–108.

2 Roger Haight, *The Experience and Language of Grace*, New York: Paulist Press, 1979, p. 21.

3 Ben Lindsay, *We Need to Talk About Race*, London: SPCK, 2019, Introduction, pp. xxv–xxix.

4 Anthony Reddie, editorial, *Black Theology* 10:3 (2012), pp. 245–50, DOI: 10.1558/ blth.v10i3.245, p. 247.

5 Rahul Rao, *Out of Time: The Queer Politics of Postcoloniality*, Oxford: Oxford University Press, 2020, p, xix.

6 Linn Marie Tonstad, *Queer Theology*, Oregon: Cascade Books, 2018, p. 31.

7 H. James Cone, *God of the Oppressed*, New York: Orbis Books, 1997, p. 34.

8 The Archbishops' Council, *Issues in Human Sexuality*, London: Church House Publishing, 1991, p. 42.

I

'This is our story, This is our song!'

Amazing grace! how sweet the sound,
That saved a wretch; like me!
I once was lost, but now am found,
Was blind, but now I see.

'Twas grace that taught my heart to fear,
And grace my fears relieved;
How precious did that grace appear
The hour I first believed!

I think it is fair to say that when people think of grace – particularly when Black folk think of grace – the song that comes to mind is the hymn that calls it 'amazing', by John Newton. Written in 1772, 'Amazing Grace' has rooted itself in the minds and hearts of Black folk – you can hear it sung by Aretha Franklin, Diana Ross, Jessye Norman, Jennifer Hudson and even Barack Obama! As a song, it communicates something of God and something of our experience of God in this world in a way that somehow manages simultaneously to evoke both a feeling of connected spirituality in Black people and a sense of collective pride and unity. What it evokes in us, I suspect, is a deep feeling of gratitude and praise to our Ancient God who has carried us over and seen us through, guided and guarded us, and brought us to where we are now even with our manifold bruises. Yet 'Amazing Grace' is also a hymn full of paradox; the dissonance being that we are, as Black people, those who have not always been protected by God from the violence of White Supremacy, of capitalism and of Christianity. We sing full of faith of the goodness of God, even as those who know what God's apparent abandonment looks and feels like. Both in our enslavement and throughout the Civil Rights

Movement to the present day, Black faith, faith that is born in the furnace of our lives, has continued singing of the goodness and grace of God in the face of so much that speaks of God's absence, betrayal and even death.

We who sing of amazing grace, despite what the world has done to us, carry an amazing faith, rooted in nothing but the promises of God whose promises are steadfast and sure. So rarely do we really interrogate the roots or history behind what we sing or even read in Church sometimes that we can find words take root in us whose origins we know nothing of. It is always a surprise to many, then, when they learn that this hymn was written by a White, Anglican priest who was born in East London and worked on three slave ships – *Brownlow, Duke of Argyle* and the *African* over a period of about five years. Eventually, 34 years after retiring from the slave trade, Newton became an abolitionist having penned the hymn 'Amazing Grace' a few years prior. It is a bittersweet thing that a hymn so loved by so many Black folk, so emblematic of our spirituality and our community, is one written by a man who participated in our dehumanization and enslavement. Now, when I sing this hymn, I can't help but think of Newton and whatever was going on in his mind and heart when he wrote the hymn. But I also find my mind thinking of all those of our African ancestors who suffered under him and his colleagues and whose names and stories we will never fully know because they lie at the bottom of the ocean, or are drowned by unrecorded history. For all my love of the hymn and what it evokes in me, nowadays I refuse to sing the words 'that saved a wretch like me'.

> wretch (noun)
> 1: a miserable person: one who is profoundly unhappy or in great misfortune
> 2: a base, despicable, or vile person[1]

The contradiction that exists here is striking. We Black folk are invited to sing of the amazing grace that we have received and yet also made to see ourselves as a wretch that has been saved by that grace. I have no idea what Newton thought we would feel singing this, but I reserve the right in this day to ensure that

I do with White people's work as I wish, and sing, read and pray those things that I find edifying and spiritually helpful. This disconnect, of course, goes beyond Newton's words – it affects every aspect of life in the Christian community because there are some who have always been made to feel like wretches in the house of God, and some who have not. As a younger person this contradiction between what the Church said and what we sung registered for me in a number of ways, and what it told us was true. I had back then, in my youth, no articulate theological grammar with which to coherently address why I found it contradictory to be both the recipient of amazing grace and a 'wretch' whom God had saved – this wretchedness could easily be located in my Blackness and my Queerness in this world and Church where both are regularly despised, discussed and contested. Although I was entirely aware of the fact that not all people were 'good' and 'holy', it was a long time before I knew for myself what sin was, and occasionally sat in church feeling I had to dig deep to find things of which to repent in the long silence our minister left during prayers of confession. I could sit and ponder – what was it, really, about my young Black Queer life that made me a 'wretch' in need of grace? And now, although this is no longer the case, I still have moments when it is easy to fall into the trappings of guilt, where the language of the Church – of the 'wretch', the 'offender', the 'unrepentant sinner' – wrap themselves around my humanity like a blanket of broken glass and hold me hostage before the liberative and redeeming God. Guilt, I have come to learn, is a fetish, and it is one that early on in our Christian formation we are made to feed on and grow accustomed to – although we sing of grace we so often feel it offered to us by the Church piecemeal and with terms and conditions that human beings have laid down in an attempt to exert power and control, and this leads to the ultimate cognitive and spiritual distortion. The Church early on in a Christian's development places itself in position as a Dom Top, and everyone, particularly those marginalized, are supposed to Bottom at any given time, submissively and without complaint. This spiritual distortion, a distortion in our relationship both to God and the Church, leaves us querying the fact that for all the evidence to the contrary in our experience of God, we are perhaps divorced from God and more frighteningly from one another. It is this sense that grace must be earned that pushes us Black LGBTQ+ folk to hide all the non-heteronormative parts of ourselves in an effort to win God's love, the Church's welcome and the pastor's favour. The same pastors who, even though they know and have preached on St Paul's words about us human beings who 'have this treasure in clay jars' (2 Corinthians 4.7), spend all their time guiding us to focus miserably on the clay-ness of ourselves and negating all the treasure. It is through them that we come to learn the very opposite of grace, through those individuals and communities who fail to accept, embrace and love us as God loves us, that we believe the lies the world tells us, and that we eventually swallow and feed on as truth. That to be queer is to give up our right to Blackness, that to be Queer is to turn our back on God, that to be queer is to choose the way of sin, the world and the devil. We know how it goes, and we know the story so well, because it is our story, and our song. It is because of this primal disconnect between our spirituality and our real lives that we begin so early on to compartmentalize a God who exists to live with us in every moment, but who we are led to believe denies us the deepest joy. It is this that forces us to leave God (at least in our minds) at the door of our bedrooms, because we cannot believe that he can be with us in moments of sexual intimacy and bodily embrace, toe-curling ecstasy and spine-tingling climax. But what happens to our spirituality, what happens to the souls of Black Queer LGBT+ folk when we believe God turns God's face away at the moments when we feel most human? What I came to discover about the Church over the years, James Baldwin the African-American playwright, essayist, activist and novelist came to discover years earlier about America:

> It comes as a great shock around the age of five or six or seven to discover that the flag to which you have pledged allegiance, along with everybody else, has not pledged allegiance to you. It comes as a great shock to discover that Gary Cooper killing off the Indians, when you were rooting for Gary Cooper, that the Indians were you. It comes as a

great shock to discover that the country which is your birth-place, and to which you owe your life and your identity, has not in its whole system of reality evolved any place for you![2]

One of my earliest memories is of Sundays and involves the Church. For so many Black Queer and trans folk, the Christian community is no stranger – we know it as intimately as we know the contours and limits of our desire. We remember the early Sunday mornings, the unchanging lateness, the watered-down squash, stale custard creams, and tea that was more milk and hot water than actual tea ...! We remember the Church aunties and uncles, the gossip and the love, the running around with our friends and being held behind while our parents caught up on a week's worth of news with their favourite brothers and sisters in the Lord. In its own special way, the joint component of all those things rendered the Church a kind of second home. It is within the walls of these buildings and in the presence of these people that we shed tears, call upon God, get slain in the Spirit, receive healing, hear God's voice and tell the Lord the burdens of our hearts. We, as Black folk, know that our churches are really trauma rooms, accident and emergency units, psychiatric wards, maternity rooms, counsel-ling spaces – that, in fact, people encounter all kinds of healing and bring all kinds of burdens to God in these spaces. We as Black folk have had an intimate relationship with the pain and suffering we come to know so well in the Jesus nailed to the cross. It is in these spaces and within this Church family that our elders found the balm that touched so profoundly the hurt-ing and tender parts of their lives and memories. I, perhaps like you, have been loved and hated by the Church, healed and hurt by the Church, encouraged and confused by the Church, enchanted and disillusioned by the Church. This makes it both a hard and a holy thing, to tell the Church how I really feel about it – in part, because the experience and the memories are neither wholly bad nor wholly good.

When Baldwin says that 'writers are obliged, at some point, to realize that they are involved in a language which they must change',[3] I realize that so much of my language has been shaped by the Christian vocabulary, that it has both given voice to my feelings and silence to my fears. When I think back now, with the lenses of honesty and maturity, I value so much of what the good parts of church life taught me. Sundays were the day when families gathered together. So many Sundays passed that involved me standing in the kitchen with a giant wooden-handled fork that looked as though it had made its way over from St Thomas, Jamaica, in someone's luggage. There I stood, turning over frying plantain as I negotiated jumping splashes of hot oil while my Nan was sitting in her bedroom peeling potatoes on her lap, watching the *EastEnders* omnibus, and my mother was listening to one of the many Jamaican artists that featured in my childhood. Essentially that meant either Capleton, Beres Hammond, Gregory Isaacs or Freddie McGregor were the background noise to my culinary efforts, if Peggy Mitchell wasn't kicking people out of her pub. Somewhere between Capleton's homophobic lyrics in 'Slew Dem' and Freddy McGregor's not wanting to be lonely was a little British-born Jamaican boy who loved Jesus but also knew he liked other boys, and later learnt he could love them too. I was, as Beres Hammond sang, 'Tempted to touch', but I had not yet known what another boy's body would do to mine, or what mine might do in another boy's embrace. That came later, and was as terrifying and magical as I had imagined.

After I'd come to terms with the fact that I would never get to lips Syed Masood and confirmed that Ben Mitchell and I had a lot in common, it wasn't long before I came to realize that both Capleton and White Christianity were not for me, in the sense that neither of them had in mind a free version of me as the Black Queer Christian that I am. At times it feels as though, if the universe had had its way, I would have certainly given up on being either openly gay or openly Christian, but I guess the universe doesn't always get its own way. When folk in church would ask me if I had a girlfriend, and old Jamaican men would encourage me during a Nine-Nights to dagger a chick next time I was raving, the paradox in my life became clearer and clearer. I, like everyone who is honest, was many things. I knew I wanted to be a priest and that rather than this being a grandiose imagining it was genuinely from God. I also knew that at that time my sexuality was anything but straightforward – was I 'into' men or 'into' women, and what the hell did any of that mean anyway? Could I be 'into' both? Could I have a same-sex partner and be ordained? Or did I have to forfeit Love in search of love. Was it possible to be gay and Jamaican? Christian and gay? Black, gay, Christian, Jamaican and proud of all four? Just as James Baldwin discovered about the flag of America and the United States, I was soon to discover that on the whole not just the Church but more specifically White Christianity, heteronormative Jamaican culture and even my own family had 'not in its whole system of reality evolved a place for [me]'.

Beyond the large hats on our grandmothers' heads, and the not-infrequent really boring preacher, church endowed us with stories, memories and family. These stories and memories embed themselves in some of our earliest recollections – such that years later, even when we have been hurt by our attempts at belonging to the Christian community, we still find ourselves enamoured by the way in which a certain hymn, Bible passage or preacher makes us feel. It is said that the Church is the place where water is thicker than blood – the place where what makes us all one family is our baptism into Jesus Christ, not our surnames. It is passing through that common water, which Christ himself passed through, that makes us one body and one faith. Although this is seldom seen to be true from where we as Black LGBTQ+ Christians are seated, I can distinctly remember having a very early sense of this as a child, brought up (quite literally) in and through the Church. Our family contained many traditions – Muslim, Atheist, Traditional African Spiritualities, and many types of Christian, both the 'born again' and the more sacramental. Family prayer times consisted of traditional versions of the Lord's Prayer and an aunt who would break out into 'shandalaboshaa' tongues midway through as if it was nothing. My grandmother who raised my sister and I was a Methodist and my grandfather a Pentecostal deacon. Our lives and rites of passage were steeped in Christianity. No one went on holiday, had surgery or attended an interview without the weight of a family prayer behind them. My grandparents both came from Jamaica in the 1960s – Nan from St Thomas and Grandad from Kingston.

It was the same Methodist Church mentioned above that put an end to my grandparents' experiment of worshipping together on arrival in the UK. The unwarranted racism of the Methodist Church forced my grandfather to worship with the Black Pentecostal Holiness folk who rented out the Methodist Church Hall in the afternoons. It was in this Methodist church that I first preached, in this church that I celebrated the Eucharist for the very first time and in this church that I preached as a Methodist in a Methodist church for the final time at my grandmother's funeral before becoming an Anglican. It was here too, in this grand yet simple Methodist church, that we heard week in and week out about the life of God. To all who came this was, now, a visibly Black church, although it only received its first Black minister once my sister and I had long grown up and left. What stuck with us most were the stories we'd heard and been taught within those walls, hallowed by prayers and tears. Stories of the Patriarchs and Matriarchs of scripture, of the Prophets and Apostles, of Jesus and the disciples – stories of the unfolding grace of God. Looking back now to those who were around us of a similar age, it is clear that so many of the people I grew up with in that church have since left the faith or chosen to practise their Christianity from home. As I left to go to train for ministry, I remember hearing reports, gossip really, of so and so who had 'gotten pregnant', 'become an addict', or basically just grown into themselves and chosen their own path. I was praised and held up for essentially having 'chosen the better way', but I still found it weird and continue to wrestle with this sense that somehow you're only worth celebrating as an adult if you've chosen the Church in a certain way. The reality of course is that God placed a call on my heart, and I've done my best to be faithful to it – but God's love for me is no more or less than it is for those who had children young, or whose marriages didn't work out, or who walked away from the faith altogether with or without 'good' reasons.

So often the Church gives us the raw material of faith, but nothing with which to navigate life when we discover the truth about ourselves, or come to realize that our identities rub up against the communities we have belonged to, leaving us in a place where we feel that our true being lives in contradiction to the faith we have been taught and given and the cultures we have inherited. I wonder what, except evil and hatred, can really be in contradiction to God's love? Can the lives of those who grow up to realize that they are attracted to people of the same sex, or that the gender assigned to them at birth isn't the gender they identify with, really be contrary to a God who in Jesus says that each and every life is precious from the first breath to the last? The Church has been for so many of us the place where we wear masks that hide our true identity, largely because we believe that God cannot handle seeing our true face, but when that mask falls off – which is part of what becoming an adult growing into the stature of Christ is all about – we realize we do not have the tools to find our feet in the faith again. This sense of being separated from our faith community and our home churches can leave us submerged in what feels like spiritual failure, a kind of failure the Church can only describe as the result of sinful weakness in one way or another. In this space we feel far from the amazing grace of God: we feel left in the state of a 'wretch'; our being made in the likeness of God is swiftly forgotten, and our relationship with our spiritual selves, even with God, can die.

About two years ago, while walking with friends at Pride in London, someone shouted at the top of their lungs in my direction: 'Priest! Oh my gosh … a priest!' I stopped and slowly turned around, at first unsure as to how this totally unexpected encounter was going to go. No one walking around in a dog collar today, given the Church's abominable reputation for sexual abuse and scandal, can be certain of a warm reception! Was this someone who thought that priests (or all Christians for that matter) really ought to know better than to be present at an LGBTQ+ affirming event? After all, such people do exist. Or, was this someone with a grudge against the Church, perhaps someone who'd had a few and wanted to 'have it out' with a 'man of the cloth'? They too exist, trust me. But no, this wasn't it at all. Instead, the person who screamed and ran over to me was a mixed-race woman in her twenties, who surrounded me with a group of equally wide-eyed and astounded friends. 'I can't believe you're here – are you, like, an actual priest?!' Once I'd assured her that I was the real deal and not in fancy dress, a conversation ensued. She poured her heart out to me. She held me, and did not let me go. I was the focus of her attention. Actually, she spoke so quickly in joy and amazement that I could hardly get my head around all that she was saying, and I kept looking at my friend in equal amounts of surprise. None of us had planned this, or imagined it. As she held me, she told me the heartbreaking story about her experiences of growing up in the Church with a knowledge deep down that she was a lesbian and wanted to be open about this. She told me what various clergy had said to her, what views her family held, and how she and her partner had been made to feel as though they had no place in the Church. Then her face lit up even more ... 'This is my partner,' she said, 'I love her so much ... our priest doesn't like it, though.' The smile vanished. 'Actually, I don't go to church any more.' And then she went quiet, held in her partner's embrace. Then, looking at me, she said, 'Are you able to give us a blessing?' At first, I hesitated. I was still choked up by the encounter, by their story, by the grace of God at work in that very moment. 'Of course,' I said, 'I'd love to!' There and then, I held them both, and God held us all, and I asked God to bless them, to comfort them and to nourish their love. It felt right, and proper, and the only adequate, albeit feeble, response to this request. When God's people are hungry, we feed them.

In every instance, the correct pastoral response is to do what Christ would do. What made this whole encounter possible were two things: first, the intersection of identities – Blackness, Queerness, Christianity – and second, our openness, presence and vulnerability in that shared space and moment. To be ordained, Black and identifiably Queer-friendly in a public space comes with risk but also opportunity. I wonder where else and in what circumstances would the woman I encountered have had her identity affirmed, her love encouraged and her existence recognized as a Black, Christian, Queer, person of colour in the UK? Which church would have had her and her partner (who was White) in mind when it seeks to be inclusive in its fellowship, mission and service? The truth is that Black LGBTQ+ Christians are far too neglected when the

Church thinks of those for whom it exists and whom it seeks to include. How many people like this person I encountered, and even my younger self, grow up unsure about God's love for us in our Black Queer Christian identities? What is so often forgotten is that it is through our enfleshed presence in places that are unfamiliar to us, or in which we are not expected to be found, that these moments of understanding, of grace and of communion become possible. It is in these moments that we realize that water can truly be thicker than blood. M. Shawn Copeland comments that human bodies are 'the medium through which the person as essential freedom achieves and realizes selfhood through communion with other embodied selves'.[4] A severe drawback in our obsession with bodies as sites of sexual misdemeanor is that it has rendered us immune to all that our flesh can teach us – we have neglected the basic human sacrament of bodily interaction as we have become imprisoned by a rupture in communion, a fear of the flesh.

As I recall that encounter at Pride, I am amazed by the sense I had in that moment of both of us recognizing the necessity, there in Piccadilly Circus, of needing to own the truths we know but can seldom name: that of our Black Queer Christian existence, of our survival, our determination, the recognition of ourselves in the story of a stranger. I, as a Christian leader, had to allow the strength of the experience I heard and encountered to touch my heart. I had to be willing to be moved by the 'other'. And pastorally, this encounter demanded of me more than mere sympathy, or a listening ear, or compassion. This was not someone 'in need' – she blessed me more than I blessed her, in fact. Rather it demanded a response of the heart not of the head, of love not of judgement, of grace and embrace. In this moment, the hip-hop idiom 'real recognize real' rang so true. Stories can be extremely powerful because of their ability to be places of honest and meaningful encounter.

When we share our story – our walk on this earth, the things we have known and seen, our hopes and fears with one another – God seems to make Godself present in a remarkable and transformational way. A large part of our story as Black Queer Christians is that we are taught, and given cues from the world around us, our families, cultures and even the Whiteness of so many LGBTQ+ spaces, to keep parts of ourselves, our stories and our true faces hidden. As those who are Black, Christian and Queer we often live feeling that so much of who we are sits in conflict with the spaces we inhabit, the families we belong to, the era we were born in. We learn too that not all 'skin folk are kin folk' as we live with the reality that those whom we might assume to be our closest allies find it impossible to embrace our Black and Queer identity. We learn that not all who are Black acknowledge the ways in which we face oppression on multiple levels, or even their part in that through their silence or through their action/inaction. We see over time the brutal reality that, in some big or small way, everyone in the world has a knee on someone's neck and it takes nothing short of maturity, self-awareness and honest courage to acknowledge and own that.

Our story as Black Queer Christians is a hard one to tell the world, because it is inherently complicated, or at least it feels that way largely because of how we are so frequently framed by a world in which Whiteness and heterosexuality are seen as the norm – consistently centred in multifarious ways and honoured, even worshipped, by the Church. We feel pressurized to choose at times between our Blackness and our Queerness, our Britishness and our Blackness, our religion and our desire, our life partner and our families, our bodies and our souls. To some we are no longer Black, to others we are no longer Christian. We live then faced with an impossible ultimatum between 'life' and life – to live as we are expected to live, or to live in the freedom that is ours but will cost us nothing short of absolutely everything to inhabit. Rarely do we see ourselves reflected in spaces that celebrate Black heritage, and we are consumed by the ever-present prevalence of White gays in what could be truly diverse and Queer spaces. How many of us have attended a Pride event only to be bombarded with a barrage of topless muscled White men who fetishize us, or are so centred in the organization of Pride that we are left questioning who the whole thing is really for?

It is because of this that UK Black Pride, Europe's largest celebration for African, Asian, Middle Eastern, Latin American and Caribbean-heritage LGBTQ people, has been so necessary.

In many ways, unlike other Pride events, UK Black Pride has maintained the momentum of something that is more than just an event, but an actual movement. Headed up by Lady Phyll Opoku-Gyimah, UK Black Pride began in 2005 when Lady Phyll and a busload of Black lesbians travelled to Southend-on-Sea for the very first event. Since then, it has provided a safe space for Black and Brown LGBTQ+ people to celebrate the joy and grace of their lives in a way that does not locate Whiteness at its centre, and is truly intersectional in its fight for inclusion and justice. In an open letter to Black LGBT people in Britain, written in 2018 ahead of UK Black Pride, Lady Phyll said these words:

On any given day, groups of people are debating your existence on the evening news. They're talking about crimes that don't affect them in places they've never stepped foot in. They're looking for you to apologize for lives you did not break and may never be able to fix. You're being judged because you look like what society thinks a man should be, but you're wearing pink lipstick. You're being ravaged by words designed to wound from the mouths of people too scared, too ignorant, and too self-absorbed to understand the harm they inflict. On any given day, someone is telling you to 'stand up straight and smile', 'all eyes are on you', 'don't embarrass your family', 'no one will take you seriously if you talk like that', 'you don't need to flaunt it in our faces, do you?', 'you were born with a dick, so you'll never be a real woman', 'go back home', 'let me check your pockets', and 'you should be grateful we allowed you in this country'. Someone is trying to free you from the oppression of Islam, save you from savages who sit in their own shit, or mansplain what feminism means. Someone who's never read bell hooks or Kimberlé Williams Crenshaw telling you intersectionality isn't a thing, that 'this isn't the Oppression Olympics'. That wanting to fight racism, sexism, homophobia and transphobia all at the same time can't be done. Taking a reprieve from the assault course of life that we know so intimately is the reason we set up UK Black Pride 13 years ago. We need spaces for ourselves. Spaces in which we can let out a collective sigh of relief. Spaces in which we're free from 'the gaze'. Spaces in which the only version of ourselves that will do, the only version of ourselves that is allowed, is the truest. Spaces in which we're protected, fought for, and celebrated. As we all know well, the necessity of safe spaces by us and for us hasn't waned, either.[5]

When I read Lady Phyll's letter, I read it with the deep knowledge that so much of what she says rings true on a significant level. The sense of the daily struggle against a world that 'on any given day' can be the perpetrator of violence on many different levels, of having to hear those who do not know what it is to walk in your shoes both discuss and decide what that walk must and might feel like, or being in spaces in which we can hardly breathe or find space for ourselves. Lady Phyll gets to the heart of what surviving in this 'assault course of life' is actually like, and how our horizons and imaginations towards freedom are regularly limited by those who say that it cannot be done, or that we are asking for too much. As a Black Queer Christian leader within the Church, reading Lady Phyll's letter and hearing how she articulates the need for spaces where Black LGBTQ+ people can be their truest selves, I also want to ponder: what if this safe space was the Church? What if the thing that cultivated and nurtured that space was the grace of God made known in Jesus? This constant sense of being in need of space within which every part of us can breathe, this sense of being invisible in the world, serves to make us feel as though we do not really exist until we are seen. Yet, we live in that difficult and sometimes tortuous space of knowing how much truly being 'seen' can cost us. As we attempt to hide our deepest, truest selves from the gaze of God, and as we protect ourselves from the gaze of Whiteness, we can suddenly find that we have not just hidden from others but from ourselves. The Black lesbian feminist Audre Lorde speaks to that sense of being made not only to choose which parts of our character to own publicly, but the sense in which that very pressured choice to present one part of ourselves as the whole is in itself a form of oppressed living, because individual sections of our identity are so often perceived as our entire being:

As a Black lesbian feminist comfortable with the many different ingredients of my identity, and a woman committed to racial and sexual freedom from oppression, I find I am constantly being encouraged to pluck out some one aspect of myself and present this as the meaningful whole, eclipsing or denying the other parts of self. But this is a destructive and fragmenting way to live.[6]

When we inhabit this destructive and fragmented way of life, the end result is that we feel seldom understood, rarely seen, and frequently invisible even to those nearest to us, even to God. In this space, cut off from owning our true identities and in the absence of those others who are like us, loneliness and isolation are inevitable. Here we yearn to see others who are like us, or as we hope one day to be – Black, Queer and free. Darnell L. Moore, in his moving memoir *No Ashes in the Fire*, expresses his own yearning to see Black Queer freedom embodied, and the power of suddenly coming to know what such freedom looks like for Black Queer and trans folk when we inhabit the world and our flesh without apology:

I needed to know that freedom looked like Black Queer and trans people fully present in their bodies, unashamed, and alive. And I needed to know Black joy was as palpable as the shared pain that comes from societal rejection.[7]

So much of the societal rejection we experience as Black Queer Christians occurs not only in the street but within our families and within our Churches. Anti-Black and anti-Queer violence so often meet in the Black Queer Christian body. Our bodies are sites of the political – pushing the contours of what society and religion deems acceptable or 'right'. Our families, the spaces in which we should know love, protection and nurture, can be sites of regulation and even abuse. We might wonder – where are we able to truly breathe? The truth is, we can find breath in one another's story. It is in the hearing and sharing of stories that we are able to witness the Black joy that is, as Darnell Moore says, 'as palpable as the shared pain' that we know all too well. Actually, the confession of our truths, our honesty and vulnerability can be acts of hospitality to one another. We can take refuge, find solace in, draw strength from, the stories of those who have lived in this world and survived despite it all. We can breathe in each other's breath as we fight and labour and love towards a world that allows us all to breathe deeply and freely. We can make space for one another in our hearts and homes and lives, as we journey towards the deeper meaning of justice in this world. We can be to each other what we need most in this world and Church, bread for the hungry, freedom for the oppressed, joy to the sorrowful, right here where grace is in famine. Simone Weil once wrote: 'Attention is the rarest and purest form of generosity.'[8] To render another our time in an undivided way allows not only for our stories to co-mingle and intertwine, but gives dignity to others in whom is the image of God. Attention is, seen another way, an act of deep love – radical, perhaps, in a world in which Black bodies are vulnerable to violence and injustice, the result of a lack of attention and the very opposite of loving generosity.

While we make space for each other in this time between our present life and the world we dream to build and are building, we need heterosexual Christians of all hues to consider Black Queer lives and the effect their theologies, commitments and behaviours have upon us. We must demand, because we are worth it, this kind of attention and space both in the Church and in society. It is this attention that encourages and motivates those who are our allies and those who may become our allies to educate and inform themselves about the kind of lives that we live and the experiences that shape our world. It is atten-tion, loving attention, which enables others to enter into the experience of those they seek to understand to a certain degree. To understand those with whom we share space in this world, we need to see them as God sees them without the longing to turn them into who we want them to be. To do otherwise is to love others only insofar as they become what we want them to become. In the words of Thomas Merton:

> The beginning of love is the will to let those we love be per-fectly themselves, the resolution not to twist them to fit our own image. If in loving them we do not love what they are,

but only their potential likeness to ourselves, then we do not love them: we only love the reflection of ourselves we find in them.[9]

In his words here, Thomas Merton touches upon precisely what I think grace is about. Grace can only truly be amazing when it ceases to seek to change the way I, and those like me, love. Grace for LGBTQ+ people is only really grace when it reaches into our love, our Blackness and our same-sex desire with gentleness, affirmation and love. An LGBTQ+ person can only make an authentic response to the message of Jesus Christ, to the Christian promise, when we are sure that that message, that person, that promise loves us as we are, not as we might otherwise be. Until we are convinced of this, any response to the gospel might be mixed with beliefs that nothing we hear Jesus say about us is really true unless we change, unless we in one way or the other, to some degree, become 'straight'. 'Straight' in this situation = holiness and purity – because the sexual sin of heterosexuals is so rarely spoken of that to escape sin in the Church today essentially means to be anything but LGBTQ+. Yet to do this, to become 'straight' and adopt patterns of heteronormative behaviour within the Church for the sake of acceptance and peace, is simply to put on a mask, because the God for whom we manifest that false change knows intimately who and what we are, and loves us despite anything we might despise about ourselves or feel awkward about. Being serious about grace sometimes means resisting forcefully the insistence from heterosexuals that LGBTQ+ Christians 'play ball' in order to be accepted or made welcome. We need to nurture a radical vision and a theology of grace that helps us fall in love with God by falling more in love with our true selves even when it makes others uncomfortable. To love ourselves to the extent that God loves us is the demand that grace makes upon us as Christians.

In order to get to this kind of love, though, we need to think about how we use language to describe ourselves and others who are children of God – language reflects our belief, contains our ideas and communicates our feelings. So often we speak about one another and indeed the world as though sin and evil were the sole defining truths about humanity. And although both have a part to play in our understanding of God and the world, when oppressed groups such as those who are Black and those who are LGBTQ+ carry the weight of these words and all that is attached to them, they not only cease to be helpful in our theology but they cease to have any meaning that leads to liberation and freedom. The Cistercian monk André Louf once said so powerfully that 'God never says to us: "I love you because you are beautiful", but "I love you because you are you, however you are …"' Heeding these words, taking them to heart, rebuilding our own self-image upon them is the work that knowing the grace of God can do in our lives. To know God's unfailing love for us is to walk and live confidently in the trust that the One who made us loves us just as we are. Anyone who seeks to know the depths of God's grace must look at Jesus Christ as the ultimate intervening reality in our world, and therefore in our understandings of one another. Jesus, the first and last word of God, whose love defines our ultimate truth and whose grace shapes the final situation of humanity, must be at the centre of all Christian dialogue because he is at the centre of the triune (Trinitarian) life of God. Grace, if it is to be truly amazing for us and in our lives, must take the love of God made known in Jesus seriously. In doing so, it offers us no half-truths or empty promises, but rather the complete fullness of life Jesus offers: freedom, liberty and peace to the LGBTQ+ Christian whoever we are, wherever we find ourselves, whatever state our life may be in. When grace is taken seriously, it centres the love of God in our interactions with each other, transforms our language and informs our attitudes. Added to this, grace, if anything, enables us to find solidarity in our humanity as those made in the image of God and journeying through this difficult life as best we can, rather than defining us as 'sinners' and 'saints'. When sin is seen as the defining truth about humanity it can very easily be treated as though it were the last word of God to and about us. Yet God does not say in the creation of the world, 'You are sinful', but we are told in Genesis that God saw what was created and declared it 'good'. It is interesting that creation is called 'good' not 'perfect'! Those who do not see and do not wish to see goodness in Black LGBTQ+ lives are unable to engage in their own sense of sin, and turn to those around them near or far who are deemed deviant and demonic – often those of us whose identities do not fit in to the heteronormative culture of Christian societies, or who authentically inhabit both our faith and the world. When this happens, LGBTQ+ people are used as scapegoats upon whose backs the total weight of a broken humanity unable to look itself in the face is placed. It is easy in these situations for communities, families, churches and cultures to point to the so-called deviant, courageous Queer people who speak the truth about their lives, what they have suffered and the locations of oppressive power, as the cause of everything falling apart, rather than for those with power and privilege to dig deeper and examine what it is that makes fear such a safe place to live. This can be even truer if you are deemed deviant because you hold a radically Black political perspective and commitment. Conservative Christians hide behind narratives that suggest that everything wrong with the Christian community lies at the feet of those who ask questions around human sexuality with open minds and hearts and who challenge the Church's institutional behaviour. Yet it is these individuals who fail to see how their failure to take the truth that every human being is made in the image of God seriously contributes enormously to the breakdown of Christian community and inhibits Christian witness in a world they are so eager to save from the fires of a hell they are certain exists but are equally certain they will never enter. What is needed is an urgent prioritizing of a theology of grace that situates grace as the primacy of God's love in every word we might say about the 'other', and that takes the crucified love of God at its word.

When we seriously examine some of the attitudes to grace that exist, we discover that, although it is a slight over-simplification, Christians in the West have understood grace essentially as pardon, rendering grace very similar in effect to mercy. This understanding locks grace into a place that speaks more of transaction than a free offer – whereas in the East, theologians have often construed grace as that which has power to heal all that isn't what it should be in our nature and as something that comes about through our participation in God and God's participation in us. The eighteenth-century Anglican priest, evangelist and leader of the Methodist movement John Wesley has been a significant influence on my own thinking around grace and salvation. Wesley's own doctrine of sanctification and grace arises primarily from his encounters with North African Christian thought, in particular the writings of St Macarius the Egyptian, St Clement of Alexandria and St Ephrem the Syrian.[10] Wesley was rooted in the Christian tradition not just of the West but also of the East, and his reading of the Church Fathers remained with him for his entire life as a prominent partner to his thinking and his intellectual arsenal for presenting a credible and attractive Christianity. For Wesley, God's grace was seen in God's goodness and wisdom, made manifest in things both great and small, from the tiniest shoot of grass to the splendour of the shining sun, a shooting star to a baby's cry – in all things God's grace and goodness were manifest and the divine image of God reflected. This grace for Wesley functioned in three ways:

- *Prevenient grace.* This is the grace of God present in all creation, which comes before any awareness on our part that it even exists. This is the grace that is in every human soul: it is the light of God in us which cannot be put out – only discovered more and more until we see it in its full depth.

- *Justifying grace.* This is the grace of God that forgives and pardons us before God and puts us into right relationship with our Creator. It is the assurance of forgiveness that comes from repentance. This is the grace that comes when we realize our identity and worth is founded only in God and God's Son, Jesus Christ, an identity that cannot be earned or taken away from us.

- *Sanctifying grace.* This is the grace of God that never stops working in us, and that seeks to bring us as close to the likeness of Jesus as possible. It is this grace that enables us to become saints, to be truly holy as God's holiness increases in us ... 'prevenient grace' continues in 'justifying grace' and is brought to fruition in 'sanctifying grace'.

In the last verse of this well-known hymn written by John Wesley's brother Charles, we see something of how grace works in us, making our hearts like Christ's heart:

Finish, then, thy new creation; pure and spotless let us be.
Let us see thy great salvation perfectly restored in thee;
changed from glory into glory, till in heaven we take
    our place,
till we cast our crowns before thee, lost in wonder, love,
    and praise.

Although we are living in the 'till' in the above verse, we often burden ourselves and others with being expected to live as those who are 'pure and spotless' children of God. Yet in this hymn we are singing about one day becoming the new creation of God, when all God's purposes are finished and fulfilled. The beauty of Wesley's theology is that while he believes in the ability of Christians to achieve true holiness in this life, and while he is committed that we strive towards it, he also holds the reality that all of us are being changed from glory into glory by various degrees in this life as we journey ever closer to eternity. None of us is the finished product, none of us is free to leave this striving behind. God in Christ works with us as we seek to live like Jesus. The issue comes when 'living like Jesus' is translated as 'no longer being Black or LGBTQ+'. Part of the reason the early Methodists were so fundamental to the abolition of the slave trade, and one of the reasons Methodism on so many social justice issues has been a forerunner in equality, is perhaps because of the emphasis the Methodist movement places on the grace of God in Christ. In describing Methodism and its message, William J. Abraham uses the image of a building with various rooms and basements, which together constitute the complex network of doctrines that became central to the movement John Wesley left behind. Abraham writes:

On entry into the spacious hallway one sees the soaring walls and the heavy pieces of classical furniture that contain the great doctrines of incarnation and Trinity developed in the early church ... Beyond that one enters a cosy living room where the guest is presented with those intimate doctrines that bring the mercy and love of God into the human heart. Downstairs in the basement there is an effective system for streaming the fresh air of grace throughout the building ...[11]

In Wesley's thinking, the all-pervasive grace of God was central to all the goodness of God witnessed in creation from its beginning to its end. The universality of God's grace echoes throughout so many Methodist hymns. In this example from Charles Wesley, an invitation is given to all God's people: the last, the least and the lost to come to the banquet of Jesus.

*Come, sinners, to the Gospel feast; Let every soul be
    Jesus' guest.
Ye need not one be left behind, For God hath bid all
    humankind.*

*Sent by my Lord, on you I call; The invitation is to all.
Come, all the world! Come, sinner, thou! All things in
    Christ are ready now.*

*The worst unto My supper press, Monsters of daring
    wickedness,
Tell them My grace for all is free. They cannot be too bad
    for Me.*

*... This is the time, no more delay! This is the Lord's
    accepted day.
Come thou, this moment, at His call, And live for Him
    Who died for all.*

Unfortunately, God's grace and the Church's handling of it has regularly turned a free gift poured out on to all into something with many terms and conditions, particularly when it comes to LGBTQ+ people. Although God's grace is freely given, 'the universal tendency of human pride is to want to turn God's covenant of grace into a contract',[12] at which point it fails to be grace. In his preaching, John Wesley was clear that grace 'does not depend on any power or merit in [humans]' nor does it depend

> on the good works or righteousness of the receiver; nor anything [they] have done, or anything [they] are. It does not depend on [our] endeavours. It does not depend on [our] good tempers, or good desires, or good purposes and intentions; for all these flow from the free grace of God; they are the streams only, not the fountain. They are the fruits of free grace, and not the root. They are not the cause, but the effects of it.[13]

Wesley is clear here that grace is not about what we have done or do, nor is it about who or what we are, rather grace is about what God has done and is doing and who God is as revealed in the life of Jesus. Wesley affirms that 'love is the very image of God: it is the brightness of his glory'.[14] Grace in us, then, doesn't depend on our being straight or married, celibate or child-bearing, masc or femme, Protestant or Catholic. Grace is all about God's love poured out on us before we know anything of it and that bears fruit in our lives and in the life of our world. The understanding of grace that Wesley holds to is evocative of the vision of abundant life given to us in chapter 55 of the book of the prophet Isaiah:

> Ho, everyone who thirsts,
>   come to the waters;
> and you that have no money,
>   come, buy and eat!
> Come, buy wine and milk
>   without money and without price.

In a world and society where everything costs us, this offer of water and food, of wine and milk, which nourish and sustain us, is counter-cultural. It is an image of God's ways of being – the God who seeks that all have abundant life pours out freely upon us those things that make life possible. Wesley put it this way:

By 'the grace of God' is sometimes to be understood that free love, that unmerited mercy, by which I, a sinner, through the merits of Christ am now reconciled to God. But in this place it rather means that power of God the Holy Ghost which 'worketh in us both to will and to do of his good pleasure.' As soon as ever the grace of God (in the former sense, his pardoning love) is manifested to our soul, the grace of God (in the latter sense, the power of his Spirit) takes place therein. And now we can perform through God, what to [ourselves] was impossible ... a recovery of the image of God, a renewal of soul after His likeness.[15]

God's grace in this understanding is free love, unmerited mercy and the power of the Holy Spirit, which contributes to our healing and our wholeness and recovers within us the image of God, renewing our souls into the likeness of God. Ultimately, God's grace is God's love – a love that is not transactional, a love that does all of the above without changing our skin colour or our sexuality or our gender into what the Church, a culture or family says it ought to be. God's grace is the understanding of God resting upon and within us, the love of God surrounding us, the power of God upholding us in our Blackness and our Queerness. Because of its ability to give us life and freedom, grace is fundamental to our life and our theology; ultimately the only thing that gives us the courage and safety to truly love all other human beings is the deep knowledge that God loves us. Any understanding of grace that doesn't express the love of God fails to communicate what grace is at its heart. Unpacking John Wesley's theology of grace, Daniel Luby says that 'for Wesley [grace] was the pardoning, transforming love of God, present to us in the indwelling of the Holy Spirit'.[16] In this sense grace is a gift given to us by God's Holy Spirit. That it comes to us through the Holy Spirit, and is embodied in the life, death and resurrection of Jesus, shows us that grace is a gift of relationship and community, a gift that cannot exist in any exclusionary sense, which cannot be reserved just for the few or stand apart from the real lives that human beings find themselves in. If we are to take seriously the fact that we are not all that we can be, we should do so without seeing our sexualities as Black LGBTQ+ people as a wrong or sinful part of our being. We should ask how it might be possible to hold the belief that we are rescued from sin by grace, and yet affirm that our salvation is not salvation from our sexuality or same-sex love. The obsessions with seeing sin as the sexual means that we fail to perceive our unjust attitudes, our greed, our hunger for power and our self-hatred as sin. God's salvation does not save us from our sexuality, our identity or our race – not only would this be impossible, but it makes no sense because neither our love nor our identities are sinful. We are saved that we might grow, in grace, into the fullness of who we are. This move from seeing our sexualities and desire as sinful to that which is loved and affirmed by God requires that we reconsider grace and interrogate it, and that we cease listening to those whose theologies seek to diminish our love and destroy our right to live as children of God.

As LGBTQ+ people, whether Christian or otherwise, we are made to view our lives and loves through the lens of sin and sinfulness. It is sin that we are introduced to light years before we hear or learn anything about grace. Whether it is the story of those two human beings that did something naughty by eating the apple of Eden (there isn't even an apple in the Bible story!) or whether it is a Sunday school lesson about Cain murdering Abel, we learn about sin in the youngest parts of our Christian experience. This is the fundamental reason why LGBTQ+ people experience a deeper sense of rupture when it comes to participation in the Church's life and inclusion within the Christian community – our identities are placed in intimate relationship with the 'sinful' without our consent and even without our knowledge. Couple that with the deep way in which darkness is demonized in so much theology and Christian language and you can see that for Black LGBTQ+ Christians there is a lot that must be undone before inhabiting Christian spirituality in a wholesome way.

This does not stop at the boundaries of language. Some LGBTQ+ Christians still are denied sacraments such as marriage, and openly LGBTQ+ clergy can be denied ordination or senior leadership positions, depending on the degree of their openness when they offer themselves to the processes of selection or attend interview. The Church demands through its inability to talk about human sexuality properly myriad compromises from LGBTQ+ Christians, and clergy in particular. The various denials of grace and the means of grace, the avenues through which God's grace is sustained and nourished in us, speak loudly to the way LGBTQ+ children of God are kept at arm's length from God's good gifts – from the 'free love' that John Wesley spoke of above. All of this makes it very difficult for us to know what grace is, means or feels like and can leave us with trust issues not only with regard to the Church but even with regard to God.

Father Patrick S. Cheng, an episcopal priest in the United States whose work has frequently focused on grace and human sexuality, says:

> Rather than starting with an autonomous definition of sin, we must start with the grace of Jesus Christ and understand sin as anything opposed to the grace of what God has done for us in Jesus Christ.[17]

I believe that changing the starting place of our dialogue is crucial, and that we must in everything start with the grace of Jesus Christ, but I also feel strongly that we must find ways to speak about our Black LGBTQ+ relationship with God, and our understanding of God by silencing some of our 'sin-talk' and allowing grace to have centre stage in our reflection on our lives. This is because grace when understood solely as forgiveness locks itself into the realm of our sinfulness. And when grace is mistaken or mixed up with mercy, it implies that someone somewhere has committed a fault or a sin. Grace is the utter outpouring of God's love; mercy, however, is always associated with the forgiveness of God, the giving of a second chance, or the kindness of a God who could choose to be other than kind. For Karl Barth, 'the starting point for thinking about sin and grace is Jesus Christ'.[18] As we'll see in the next chapter, our understanding of Jesus is the key to our understanding not only of grace as embodied in Christ's life and in the life of God, Father, Son and Holy Spirit, but Jesus is the key to our understanding the entirety of Christian theology. It is interesting that

'Barth understands sin as whatever is opposed to the grace of what God has done for humanity in Jesus Christ'.[19] By extension, those who oppose the work of God's grace as being alive and fruitful in the lives of Black LGBTQ+ people commit sin by failing to look for God's grace in us. We should perhaps apply to homophobia the kind of weight applied to us with regard to homosexuality, and challenge the amount of 'grace' shown to those who claim to follow Jesus yet who continue to exclude God's children from his loving-kindness and the body of God's Son, the Church. Those who seek to understand and engage with the Black LGBTQ+ communities must realize that in Jesus we are all of us one body, despite our differences. This means that 'grace requires a commitment to changing how we see and interact with the world'.[20]

If the language around sin and grace is to cease doing Black LGBTQ+ lives harm, we must reclaim these terms, understand their place in the colonizer's mind, the history of Christianity and the theologies that have shaped the Church in recent times, and redefine their use. It is not that the doctrine of sin has no relevance, but that its relevance regarding life appears to fall solely upon LGBTQ+ lives in a Church that has more to say about gay sex and gender transition than institutional abuse and social injustice. Black LGBTQ+ Christians spend their lifetimes contemplating the doctrine of sin even if they cannot name it, and sometimes questioning their salvation in the context of a culture and Church reluctant to contemplate why it has treated Black LGBTQ+ bodies in the way it has and continues to. The way the Church talks about sin in relation to LGBTQ+ people affects our emotional, spiritual, physical and psychological well-being. It can affect people's ability to respond to their vocations, their ability to fall in love or sustain a relationship, their work and family lives, their friendships. To grow up with a sense of self-hatred founded upon your understanding of God is to quite literally grow up with a world turned upside down, a world within which you can never quite make sense. Patrick Cheng makes a powerful case for why we ought to reconsider grace. Yet, I find I struggle with his definition of grace as 'an amazing gift from God that helps us to be reunited with God after a period of separation'.[21]

I wrestle with the definition in part because I wrestle with the notion that anyone can truly be separated from God, and on a deeper level I feel as though it situates grace in a way that says that those who receive it are primarily flawed or, in this case, 'separated' from God when so many of us have felt ourselves distanced from God through no fault of our own. Cheng also invokes the language of 'no longer [being] the people we once were', having come into contact with God's grace. Seeing grace as something that is transformational is good, as grace really does change our lives for the better, but the language of no longer being who we once were is deeply disturbing as a Black LGBTQ+ person. In all of our preaching and teaching in the Christian community we need to be cautious about how the language of this transformation lands on those who still see their sexuality as in need of further transformation and change. Grace, of course, makes demands upon each of our lives as individuals and as communities. However, this transformation leads us into our authentic selves, rather than away from them. It affirms our kinky hair and Queer sexualities, and gives us the confidence to be ourselves rather than the fear that insists we become less ourselves.

Dietrich Bonhoeffer, a Lutheran Pastor and anti-Nazi dissident, when speaking about grace challenged people to think through what kind of grace is offered to us by God in Christ. He makes a differentiation between costly grace and cheap grace. He says in relation to cheap grace that it 'is the deadly enemy of our Church ... Cheap grace is grace without discipleship, grace without the cross, grace without Jesus Christ, living and incarnate.'[22] Although Bonhoeffer is making the argument for grace requiring some change or transformation in the lives of those who seek to follow Jesus, it is interesting to use his idea of cheap grace as a way to define the kind of grace homophobic and transphobic Christians make use of to disregard their negative attitudes towards us. Too often fundamentalist Christians see the LGBTQ+ community as the place most urgently in need of transformation by the Holy Spirit, to the degree that they fail to see the need for their own transformation and repentance. Such people hold to a doctrine of costly grace, particularly with regard to women deemed sexually immoral and anyone who identifies as LGBTQ+ or even those who happen to be working that out. Conservative Christians never seem to experience the kind of transformation that enlarges their capacity to love those different from them, or the kind of transformation that enables them to stand with us as allies rather than against us. LGBTQ+ people are expected to manifest all kinds of transformations (even those scientifically impossible), while those are off the cards for the people who oppose our existence. It might be easy to suggest that my own theology of grace, or the theology I am working towards – one that enables Black LGBTQ+ Christians to live freely and openly, and demands nothing of Black LGBTQ+ Christians except that they love God and love themselves – is one of 'cheap grace'. But as grace is treated currently within the Church, it is ceasing to be 'amazing' for Black Queer Christians and is used cheaply by those who demand that grace costs the LGBTQ+ person nothing short of everything. If grace is, as I believe, the trustworthy friendship of a good God, then it must be reconsidered in such a way that it motivates all Christians to welcome, love and accept all other Christians. Grace is the persistence of a loving-kindness that makes no worldly sense. It is the inexhaustible, unbounded and unmerited love God made known in Jesus Christ and from which not one human being is excluded. How amazing is grace if it fails to extend this love to every corner of our human experience, every inch of our desire and longing, every aspect of our physical and spiritual need? We need Christians to move to a place of understanding the love of God and the LGBTQ+ community to such a degree that all their strength and love are put around us, so that we might live life in all its fullness alongside them.

The British BAFTA award-winning actress, screenwriter and producer Michaela Coel, known particularly for her performances and writing of *Chewing Gum* and more recently *I May Destroy You*, gave a breathtakingly profound MacTaggart Lecture in 2018. It was both prophetic and courageously honest. As a screenwriter she has frequently captured much of the experiences of young Black Britons, but particularly the Black Queer Christian community. She says:

New bonds replaced lost ones upon finding myself in a
church. I fell in love with God, with 'Jesus'; his actions, his
character. I read the Bible and loved its metaphors, its *hope*,
it's what propelled me into becoming a poet.[23]

She then goes on to speak about her experience in the Church
and how it shaped her, and indeed her attitudes to others:

As an Evangelical Christian, the plan was to teach the homo-
sexuals about Jesus, but I accidentally ended up becoming
best friends with some and learning from these other kinds
of misfits. *Yes*, homosexual bonds replaced biblical ones. I
still love the character of Jesus. I just started paying attention to the stuff written *around* Him, written by people who
knew how to write, and didn't care for what I read.[24]

How many Christians see their role as 'teaching' LGBTQ+
Christians about Jesus? How many Christians come into encounter with LGBTQ+ Christians open to encountering something of Jesus in our midst? What Michaela Coel experienced
was a transformation of her vision not just of LGBTQ+ people
but of her own role in relationship to us. This transformation
has enabled her to portray something of our lives in her work
that is true, affirming and beautiful. Michaela Coel creates
from her own sense of knowing that God is not synonymous
with safety something that Black LGBTQ+ Christians live with
in daily life – it is not easy to take God at her word, and believe
that we are made in God's image.

When we sing 'through many dangers, toils and snares',
we are often aware that that includes this world, our families,
workplaces and even our spiritual communities. Despite all it
costs us in our attempts at belonging, the Church enters into
the deepest parts of our imagination, and the Christian story
shapes our work and living. Despite being gay, and having left
the Church, James Baldwin remained fascinated and rooted in
Christianity's language. When he recalls the Church, he does
so with a sense of joy and love:

The Church was very exciting. It took a long time for me to disengage myself from this excitement, and on the blindest, most visceral level, I never really have, and never will. There is no music like that music, no drama like the drama of the saints rejoicing, the sinners moaning, the tambourines racing and all those voices coming together and crying holy unto the Lord. There is still, for me, no pathos quite like the pathos of those multicoloured, worn, somehow triumphant and transfigured faces, speaking from the depths of a visible, tangible, continuing despair of the goodness of the Lord. I have never seen anything to equal the fire and excitement that [could] sometimes, without warning, fill a church, causing the church ... to 'rock'. Nothing that has happened to me since equals the power and the glory that I sometimes felt when, in the middle of a sermon, I knew that I was somehow, by some miracle, really carrying, as they said, 'the Word' – when the church and I were one. Their pain, their joy were mine, and mine were theirs – they surrendered their pain and joy to me, I surrendered mine to them – and their cries of 'Amen!' and 'Hallelujah!' and 'Yes, Lord!' and 'Praise His name!' and 'Preach it brother!' sustained and whipped on my solos until we all became equal, wringing wet, singing and dancing, in anguish and rejoicing, at the foot of the altar. It was, for a long time ... my only sustenance, my meat and drink. I rushed home from school, to the church, to the altar, to be alone there, to commune with Jesus, my dearest Friend, who would never fail me, who knew all the secrets of my heart.[25]

If we, as Black LGBTQ+ Christians, are ever to meet our dearest friend, the one who never fails us and who knows all the secrets of our hearts but loves us anyway, we will need to trust in the grace of God. We will have to resist being pushed into heteronormative ways of being, resist hiding our Queerness from God, and embrace our Blackness in all its beauty. If as Black LGBTQ+ Christians we are to live life in all its fullness we must go on telling our story and singing our song – until all the voices of God's family sing it with us. Between now and then, we have to trust in the promises of God, which neither fail nor crumble – the God who made us just as we are, and who loved us into being, the God who from our first breath to our last cradles us in a loving and accepting embrace.

> *The Lord hath promised good to me,*
> *His word my hope secures;*
> *He will my shield and portion be*
> *As long as life endures.*

> *When we've been there ten thousand years,*
> *Bright shining as the sun,*
> *We've no less days to sing God's praise*
> *Than when we first begun.*[26]

Notes

1 www.merriam-webster.com/dictionary/wretch, accessed 16.3.21.

2 James Baldwin, debate with William Buckley at the Cambridge Union, 1965, www.youtube.com/watch?v=5Tek9h3a5wQ, accessed 1.3.21.

3 James Baldwin, 'On Language, Race and the Black Writer', http://marktwainstudies.com/wp-content/uploads/2017/02/Baldwin-1979-.pdf, accessed 1.3.21.

4 M. Shawn Copeland, *Enfleshing Freedom: Body, Race, and Being*, Minneapolis: Fortress Press, 2010, p. 24.

5 Phyll Opoku-Gyimah, *Open Letter to Black LGBT People in Britain and Beyond Ahead of UK Black Pride 2018*, https://www.blackhistorymonth.org.uk/article/section/letters/open-letter-black-lgbt-people-britain-beyond-ahead-uk-black-pride-2018/, accessed 1.3.21.

6 Audre Lorde, 'Age, Race, Class, and Sex', in *Sister Outsider*, New York: Random House, 2007. p. 210.

7 Darnell L. Moore, *No Ashes in the Fire: Coming of Age Black and Free in America*, New York: Nation Books, 2018.

8 Letter to Joë Bousquet, 13 April 1942; Simone Pétrement *Simone Weil: A Life*, trans. Raymond Rosenthal, New York: Pantheon Books, 1976.

9 Thomas Merton, *No Man Is An Island*, New York: Harcourt Brace, 1955.

10 A. D. Wood, *The Burning Heart*, Lexington: Emeth Press, 2007, p. 43.

11 William J. Abraham, *Methodism: A Very Short Introduction*, Oxford: Oxford University Press, 2019, pp. 41–2.

12 James Torrance, 'The Theological Grounds for Advocating For-giveness and Reconciliation in the Sociopolitical Realm', in Daniel Philpott (ed.), *The Politics of Past Evil*, Notre Dame: University of Notre Dame Press, 2006, p. 48.

13 John Wesley, 'Sermon on Free Grace, preached at Bristol in the year 1740', para. 3.

14 Albert C. Outler (ed.), *The Works of John Wesley*, vols 1–4, *Sermons*, Nashville: Abingdon Press, 1984–87, 4:355.

15 Randy L. Maddox, *Responsible Grace: John Wesley's Practical Theology*, Nashville: Kingswood Books, 1994, p. 85.

16 Daniel Luby in Maddox, *Responsible Grace*, p. 120.

17 Patrick Cheng, in Kelly Brown Douglas and Marvin M. Ellison (eds), *Sexuality and the Sacred*, Louisville: Westminster John Knox Press, 2010, p. 106.

18 Ibid., p. 107.

19 Ibid., p. 108.

20 Ibid., p. 110.

21 Patrick Cheng, *From Sin to Amazing Grace: Discovering the Queer Christ*, New York: Seabury Books, 2012, p. 24.

22 Dietrich Bonhoeffer, *The Cost of Discipleship*, New York: Touchstone, 1995, pp. 43–5.

23 www.broadcastnow.co.uk/broadcasters/michaela-coel-mactaggart-lecture-in-full/5131910.article, accessed 16.3.21.

24 Ibid.

25 Toni Morrison, *James Baldwin's Collected Essays*, New York: Library of America, 1998, p. 306.

26 John Newton, 'Amazing Grace', written in 1772 and published in 1779.

2

Grace Enough for Thousands?

Grace is a powerful message to hear: that the cost of salvation is nothing.

Lenny Duncan, *Dear Church*[1]

Queer Black Christian LGBTQ+ lives matter. More importantly, they matter to God. God loves Black Queer LGBTQ+ people wherever we fall under or between those labels, and even when we resist or despise them. God loves us, God loves our lives, God loves our being – because we, all of us, belong to God. To say this should not seem radical or particularly new, but, for so many of us, hearing it is. This may be the first time a Church leader has said that your life has worth, meaning and value to God – and yet this is the whole point of a thing called grace. Grace is the undeserved, inexhaustible and unconditional love of God embodied in Jesus Christ. Grace enables us to see ourselves as God truly sees us, rather than the way we are made to see ourselves through the lenses of the world, our histories, our families, or even those who might wish us harm. To be Queer, Black and Christian is to know the precarious nature of our existence both within society and particularly within the Christian community. We who identify as LGBTQ+ are at constant risk of theological violence as well as ecclesial terror. Our lives suffer the rupture of being made to feel inherently incoherent, even paradoxical and contradictory. We are not, in our Black Queer identity, afforded the illusionary comforts of power and privilege, but rather we exist as those who live somewhere between hope and faith in a world that requires daily courage and perseverance just in order for us to survive in our Queer Blackness. In a world that does not want us to breathe, at least not publicly, we are warriors in what feels often like a lifelong battle for air. As people of faith, we have often come to understand something of God either because of the contexts in which we have first learnt about God or because of what is said about God to us by others. For many who identify as Black Christian and LGBTQ+, God is perceived as that which is unrelated, superior to or uninterested in us as whole, feeling, integrated beings. We mature as those who have on the whole been made to believe that in order to experience the divine, and in order to enter churches, we have to meet certain standards in language, behaviour and aesthetic. I have to dress up for God, use the right language with God, be desire-less, disembodied and not quite whole in the presence of God. I cannot be mad with God, doubt God or even question God. God is the one to whom I am made to wear a mask, or many, and God is rendered simultaneously fragile and ruthless. God is that of which I am afraid and yet also the one whose perfect love casts out all fear, God is my creator and my sustainer – the Shepherd I shall not want, but also it seems 'He' (and it's almost always put this way) who can reduce me to absolutely nothing. God is the one from whom I hide my deepest self; my wounds, my fragility, my fears and longings. Yet we are told in the same breath that God is the one who made us, and who knows us as we truly are. For many, we may even imagine that God is in fact disgusted by us, and yet God is a God of relationship, a God who in God's very nature longs for community and love and equality with all that God has created. You can see that as Black LGBTQ+ Christians we live with myriad ideas and images of God, and in that we are not alone. What makes our experience of God distinct is that our image of God is narrowed by the Church's historic and present-day overemphasis on LGBTQ+ sin, such that for us the last thing we often understand God to be is our friend, and if we come to that understanding we often enter into that friendship having left our sexuality behind.

I am committed to an understanding of God that sets God free from the place of judgement and wrath in which Black LGBTQ+ people have become so accustomed to approaching God. God is a God of love and grace, both of which are undeserved, unmerited and unconditional. Although we might not always realize it, love always begins with an encounter – it cannot be theorized, met or understood in mere words. Love must be enfleshed. To make sense of this I like to go back to the first few pages of the scriptures. In Genesis 1.26–27 we read of a God who exists not in the lofty heights of heaven, removed from humankind, but in relationship with Godself and who brings us into being out of that first family of Father, Son and Holy Spirit, what Christians call the Trinity:

> Then God said, 'Let us make humankind in our image,
>   according to our likeness ...
> So, God created humankind in his image,
>   in the image of God he created them.

The 'us' we hear of in Genesis 1.26–27, we can imagine, is God as the Church has historically named God – as that Trinitarian life, one God in three persons: Father, Son and Spirit. It is this God: Creator, Redeemer, Sustainer, who at the beginning of time exists not in solitude and separation but in relationship, in community – one who seeks to further that community and extend that family by creating humankind. You and I, as we are, have our existence from this first community, this first union of the three persons of God who exist together from before all things. This means that no one truly stands 'alone' or in isolation. We are not only connected to one another but we find our 'home', our origin, in the Trinitarian life of God. As God's children we are made in God's image, and we are part of God's life – because God existed before us as that love from which all that is loved flows. What does this reveal to us about God's nature and our place in the biblical story? It tells us that God is a God for whom interconnectedness, community, fellowship and relationship are part of God's nature, simply part of God's way of being. God's love for you is not God 'going the extra mile' to be super kind, or to make you feel good – it is God being God. But more than that, that God who creates does so in God's image and likeness. God doesn't make us as something that has no connectedness to Godself – God creates us in such a way that we cannot truly exist outside of God. This means that all people, whoever they are, whatever their identity, whether they have discovered the other side of the closet or are firmly sheltered within it, carry something of God's blueprint, God's 'DNA' within them. When I look at you, and when you look at me, we are invited to see – in fact, we are challenged to see – something of the image and likeness of God.

This claim, that people are made in God's image and likeness, implies that no human being – indeed, no human life – can be redundant to either Christian communities or, more fundamentally, to God and to society. The fourth-century bishop, St Gregory of Nyssa (born in present-day Turkey), wrote regarding the image of God: 'It dwells within every one of us, ignored and forgotten.'[2] As Black LGBTQ+ Christians, we experience the world and the Church in a way that communicates to us the degree to which the image of God within us remains ignored and forgotten. We should ask then, whenever we doubt our true worth, would it make sense for God to invest Godself in the effort of creating only to be willing to throw that which reflects Godself away? What would it mean if God, having created us in God's likeness, did not love that which is created (you and me) as a reflection of the God who creates, only because that is what love does – it gives itself away? All this is to say that when we are made to feel redundant to God, it simply doesn't make sense in relation to God having made us in the first place. Love gives life, gives hope, gives joy – and we see this not only in nature, where in so many cases animals nursing their young will do all they can to sustain the life of their offspring, but we see this too in the revelation of God in Jesus, who through the cradle and the cross gives his life for the world.

Understandably, this can seem like a bizarre place to begin reflecting on Black Queer Christian identity, but to start anywhere else seems to me to set off on the wrong foot. I want to start here with what I feel should colour every other aspect of our thinking as those who are Black LGBTQ+ and Christian, as well as those who might already be or are considering becoming our allies. We need to think through our theologies of God, and how our theology of God impacts our understanding of each other. To ask who God is for us is to begin to see who we think God ought to be for others. If God can accept me, then maybe God can accept you too. If God can embrace the paradoxes of my life, perhaps God is not allergic to paradox in our collective lives. If God's grace can be active in my life, my community, my context, then maybe I should seek to see that same grace of God in places beyond my own fields of understanding, comfort and experience. All of this is part of the work that grace fulfils in the minds and hearts of those who seek God. But what is grace, and how do we come to know and receive it?

In order for us to understand grace (and whether we ever really can understand it is a question worth considering) we must look at the life of Jesus Christ. In looking at Jesus we come to know not only who God is but what God is like. It is in how Jesus moves among us as people in this world, in the things he has said and done, the places in which he placed himself, that we come to catch a glimpse of the character of God in the fullness of Jesus. So scripture, and the Gospels in particular, speak to us of God's grace, in as much as they hold the story of God's action in the world and particularly God's action in Jesus Christ for us. Fundamentally, grace is a gift – that which brings human beings from their various walks of life and identities into intimacy with God's life. Peter Groves puts it this way:

> Grace is the word we use to describe God's infinite love worked out in human beings by drawing those human beings into the perfect fellowship of the Trinity, the eternal selfless love of Father, Son and Holy Spirit ... to receive the grace of God is to be invited into God's own self.[3]

This gift of course has an origin to which we must look if we can truly accept and appreciate the fullness of this gift. At the heart of the Christian story is a people who live and wait in darkness with longing, uneasy and hungry hearts. They are waiting and longing for that which they cannot name, or imagine. The prophet Isaiah writes:

> *The people who walked in darkness*
> *have seen a great light;*

those who lived in a land of deep darkness –
on them light has shined.

Isaiah 9.2

These people are awaiting a Saviour, one who would come to bring peace, comfort, harmony, justice, joy and healing. Yet none could know that these things would come not in the form of a great and powerful ruler or prince or king, in the earthly sense, but in a small, helpless and vulnerable child. At the heart of the Christian message is this birth – of one small baby in whose arrival everything is turned upside down. God enters the world in Christ through an opening between urine and faeces, having been carried in the womb of Mary and delivered into the world just like the rest of us. God's solidarity with humankind is seen in this, that Jesus the Son of God is born among us, to us, as one of us to show us what God is like. In Luke's Gospel the mother of this child, Mary, sings a song of a new vision of creation in which she says that God has

> scattered the proud in the thoughts of their hearts ... brought down the powerful from their thrones, and lifted up the lowly ... filled the hungry with good things, and sent the rich away empty.
>
> Luke 1.51–53

In this song, offered up to God from a previously unknown village girl who now was the handmaid of God, we witness the kind of radical vision that an encounter with God brings. Mary's vision is united with the vision of Jesus, her child, who in his life and through his saving work on the cross will scatter the proud, bring down the powerful from their thrones, fill the hungry and send the rich away empty. The child she bore in her womb has come into the world not to live for his own sake but to draw all people to himself, that they might see themselves as God sees them. This story that we recall at Advent and at Christmas of the birth of Christ takes us to the heart of one of the major claims of Christianity: that God was made flesh, made human, in Jesus Christ and that the birth of this child changes everything. The word that theologians use for this quite-difficult-to-comprehend concept is the 'incarnation', and it is this, the doctrine of God becoming human, that makes Christianity a unique faith among many of the world's religions. Of course, it is a bold and courageous statement to make, to say and believe that the great, grand architect of the universe – God – has become human; yet this is what the Church teaches. Christian doctrine (what the Church teaches as truth) has consequences, however, and so the claim of the incarnation affects many aspects of Christian life and practice. For example, if the baby born in Bethlehem is God-made-flesh, then how that child comes into the world must be special too. If the one who bore him for nine months before his birth was a virgin, she too must be special. And so this doctrine that we might think is all about Jesus Christ has something to say too about those around him, the one who brings him into the world, and about those who call him Lord and Saviour. Ultimately, the birth of Jesus says something about you and me. The North African bishop, St Athanasius of Alexandria, makes this point quite beautifully when he says:

> speaking of the manifestation of the Saviour to us, it is necessary also to speak of the origin of human beings, in order that you might know that our own cause was the occasion of his descent and that our own transgression evoked the Word's love for human beings, so that our Lord both came to us and appeared among human beings. For we were the purpose of his embodiment, and for our salvation he so loved human beings as to come to be and appear in a human body.[4]

This event, the birth of Christ, while only marked by most people on one day of the year, is, I want to suggest, the most important event in the church year and fundamentally important to those of us who are Black, Christian and LGBTQ+. The event of Christ's birth should not be seen as a moment in history that we call to mind just once a year, either as the Church or wider society. Beneath the tinsel and the Christmas wrappings, beneath the carols and trees, there is real flesh in the manger of Bethlehem, and that flesh is God. If we are to understand the grace of God, we must be willing to see the story of Jesus' birth in all its fullness as opposed to its 'feel-good' all-too-commercialized factor. God is doing serious business in the birth of Jesus in Bethlehem and it is more profound than any Christmas card or nativity play can tell. Rather, the birth of Jesus is the climax of God's seeking out of those who live at the margins of society, the companionship of God with those who do not have a place in which to be born; with refugees, the homeless and asylum seekers, the birth of Jesus is the solidarity of God alongside those whose lives are fragile from the very moment of birth and who die before they live due to the brutality of people, policies and governments. Jesus being born of Mary is God standing alongside all women whom society fails to see, whose stories of pregnancy might not add up, who have visions for a new world, and who carry songs waiting to be set free in their hearts. To those who live in fear and walk in darkness, to those yearning for hope and hungry for love, to those restricted to the boundaries of the closet and who dare not speak the truths they know but are too afraid to name, God, in Christ says just what he said to Mary in the voice of the angel Gabriel: 'Do not be afraid.'[5]

The birth of Jesus, and God's coming to us in Jesus, is the antidote to fear. Jesus Christ entering the world all those years ago says something to those of us today who might feel as though our lives and our existences do not matter, who despise the flesh we live in and are shunned by the communities we inhabit. Whatever stories we carry, and whatever narratives we might run from, in being born all those years ago, Jesus lives our stories with us as God made human. What is very easy to overlook is that there was a time when God was not named, and when God's name fell silent.[6] In the book of Exodus, recounted for so many and imprinted in our minds thanks to the animation *Prince of Egypt*, we see Moses, who, in the third chapter of Exodus, encounters God in the burning bush. God knows Moses by name and repeatedly calls him: 'Moses, Moses!' Eventually, afraid and having hidden his face, Moses asks God who God is and the voice replies: 'Eyheh-Asher-Eyheh' – 'I am who I am'. Later, God continues to identify as 'the Lord, the God of your ancestors, the God of Abraham, the God of Isaac, and the God of Jacob', and says that is his name. Moses' experience of God is both terrifying and fairly anonymous in terms of name, God is faceless and overpowering, a contrast to the little baby born and full of vulnerability in the manger of Bethlehem. In Jesus, God becomes a reality who can be invoked. The name of God is no longer something towards which we grasp, it becomes the flesh of our flesh and bone of our bone – God in Christ is one with us. In Christ, God is named and dwelling among us, standing in coexistence with each child of God.[7]

So it is that we must wrestle with this enormous reality at the heart of the Christian faith. That God becomes flesh in Jesus, and God does all of that so that we might live in intimacy with him. St Gregory of Nazianzus speaks of God becoming human in Jesus as something that is purely motivated by love, and which occurs 'that the ungraspable might be grasped'.[8] Christ's birth is God placing Godself beside us in this world, it is God emptying Godself of everything but love so that we might see the love his face has to offer us, and hear the fluency of his mercy in the voice and words of Jesus. The claims we make about God deeply affect us, and the God we see revealed in Jesus – in his vulnerability, his humility, his gentleness and willingness to give his life for us on the cross – says that God is vulnerable, humble, gentle and selfless.

In the words of Dietrich Bonhoeffer, what we see in the birth of Jesus is that:

God becomes human, really human. While we endeavor to grow out of our humanity, to leave our human nature behind us, God becomes human, and we must recognize that God wants us also to become human – really human. Whereas we distinguish between the godly and the godless, the good and the evil, the noble and the common, God loves real human beings without distinction ... God takes the side of real human beings and the real world.[9]

If Bonhoeffer is right, that God becomes human for us, and in so doing longs for us not only to become human but 'really human', might we see this in the life that Jesus lives? A life that, from the cradle to the cross, speaks of authentic love and sacrifice, of mercy and justice, of grace and truth. In essence what Bonhoeffer points us to is what we might call our true vocation (our calling and purpose in life). Our deepest vocation, our truest purpose, is not to become less human but *really* human. And if Jesus models for us what real humanity is, our vocation in life is to be like him. Between the brokenness of our lives and our weaknesses, there is this thing called grace that Jesus reveals and in himself embodies. Grace, Peter Groves writes,

> is the love of God at work, uniting human beings with Jesus Christ, the second person of the Trinity incarnate, and drawing them into fellowship with him. It is not neat and tidy, not polite and withdrawn, but gently and relentlessly aggressive, offending us with its inclusion and undermining our securest assumptions about that which we think we know to be true.[10]

To me, grace is powerful because, rather than enabling me to see myself through the lenses of any other human being, it enables me, or at least passionately invites me, to see myself through the loving gaze of God. It is through this gaze that we come to see ourselves as loved, worthy of love and capable of loving. It is this primal love flowing from the very heart of God towards us that enables us to see beyond what our eyes see and to listen beyond what our ears hear – beckoning us to consider a future in which we enter into and inhabit what might be called a 'graced' life. As those who are so often made to see ourselves through the lens of our sexuality before all else, a sexuality that we have often been taught is inherently sinful, to see ourselves as God *truly* sees us is the work of a lifetime. It is to that work, however, that God calls us. God in Jesus Christ is encouraging us to look at ourselves anew – through the eyes of God rather than just our own. God in Jesus Christ calls us to live an authentic life, in which we know ourselves to be loved and lovely as those who are held and valued by the God who has created us and called us into being – just as we are. Ultimately, shame, secrecy and sin will always be abundant wherever grace is in famine ... wherever we do not allow grace to have the loudest voice in our minds and hearts, the voices that tell us that we are not enough will speak loudest.

As children of God, we must not wait for death to live the life that God has created us for. In our Black LGBTQ+ joy, with those who have come before us, we know what it means to defy the odds – we create and have created spaces in which grace becomes possible even before we understand what grace is. As those who know more deeply what the famine of grace is, we make grace flow abundantly, as together we nourish each other into the fullness of the freedom of God's love. Whether we are considering coming out of the closet, owning a name we feel is truly ours, or leaving behind the gender identity we feel we do not recognize, to live a graced life means living in the deepest authenticity we can – not just because it is our right, but because that is what God calls us to in Jesus. As the poet George Wade Robinson wrote in his hymn 'I Am His and He Is Mine':

Loved with everlasting love,
Led by grace that love to know;
Spirit, breathing from above,
Thou hast taught me it is so.
Oh, this full and perfect peace!
Oh, this transport all divine!
In a love which cannot cease,
I am His, and He is mine.

The culmination, the climax, of God's grace-action is evidenced in the life we see in Jesus from his birth to his death and his resurrection. We find God in the shape of Jesus, who lives as the proximity of God to us in the midst of our world. In his death and resurrection, what is often referred to as his 'passion', we see Jesus modelling for us the very paradox of the values seen so often in our world. In Jesus willingly going to the cross, sharing in our Black reality where betrayal, injustice, police brutality and trauma are all too familiar, Jesus aligns himself not with the strong and powerful but with the oppressed, the suffering, the rejected. The cross, like the lynching tree and indeed the very pavements of Ferguson,[11]

Minneapolis[12] and Eltham,[13] becomes a site of public Black and Brown death. Jesus dies an unjust, brutal and public death – not because of any crimes committed but by virtue of who and what he was, and the claims he made about the radical love of God. He was crucified by the ruthless powers of Empire, put to death because crowds turned into mobs and a culture of violence called for his blood, and while those closest to him fled for the safety of their own lives, Mary his mother stood where so many Black women have stood – weeping over their prematurely dead babies, their brutalized boys and girls in a climate empty of justice and peace. The life of Jesus and the life of Mary are lives of solidarity with the suffering people of the world, with the LGBTQ+ communities who experience societal and theological violence, and injustice under the law, in so many parts of the world – even in what some refer to proudly as 'Christian' cultures.

Both Mary and Jesus model for us the kind of solidarity that all the suffering can have with each other – the standing side by side with those condemned to stoning, those who are crucified and those who are vilified in our world. Jesus is the joy of God, the solidarity of God, the love of God made flesh. We see the joy, solidarity and love of God at work in the death and resurrection of Jesus – not only in Christ's sacrifice on the cross for the life of the whole world, but in the very fact that, out of love for us, God refuses to allow the Empire to have the last word. Instead, God's love and grace shine anew in the darkness of the tomb – God's love and grace not only overcome death but embrace it, and transform even death into that which for us has the possibility of new life. What for the disciples appeared as a moment of eternal grief becomes the source of their deepest and unending joy. It can be all too easy when reflecting on our own lives as Black Queer Christians to focus on the suffering and challenges, but we too are called to look beyond our own personal cross. At the centre of our lives there are also moments of sudden and endless joy – Black Queer joy – moments of grace and love.

To return at the close of this chapter to where we began – we come to contemplate the enormity of the incarnation. One particular way in which we might think about Jesus, the word of God made flesh, is to see Jesus as the joy of God in whom all of history comes together as our Saviour, Redeemer and Friend. Jesus forgives our pasts, heals our brokenness and sustains us in and through his grace. We must take seriously and root ourselves in the reality that Jesus came not only to give us life but life in all abundance (John 10.10). What Jesus offers us from the cradle to the cross, and still today, is unending joy. Wherever that joy is absent, grace may be in famine. Jesus is the joy of those who know they are loved and valued by God – a joy that cannot be taken away because it is as permanent as God's love. It is Jesus who is God's fellowship with us, Jesus who is the one in whom we come to know intimacy with God – Jesus who makes hope possible because in his incarnation we find that 'deep, sympathetic communion'[14] that is God's solidarity with all humankind and particularly those who know the pain of discrimination and suffering. It is Jesus who is the lover of Black Queer Christians, Jesus who calls us by name, and Jesus who reminds us through his body of the love of the Father and the Son and the Spirit. In the birth, death and resurrection of Jesus what we see embodied for us, just as we are, is the grace of God – that grace of God which says that what is important in Christian life is not so much our journey to God but God's journey to us.

Father of all,
we give you thanks and praise,
that when we were still far off
you met us in your Son and brought us home.

Dying and living, he declared your love,
gave us grace, and opened the gate of glory.
May we who share Christ's body live his risen life;
we who drink his cup bring life to others;
we whom the Spirit lights give light to the world.

Keep us firm in the hope you have set before us,
so we and all your children shall be free,
and the whole earth live to praise your name;
through Christ our Lord.
Amen.[15]

Notes

1 Lenny Duncan, *Dear Church: A Love Letter from a Black Preacher to the Whitest Denomination in the US*, Minneapolis: Fortress Press, 2019, p. 26.

2 Gregory of Nyssa, *Restoring God's Image* (On Virginity, 46.369B–376B), in Herbert Msurillo SJ, *From Glory to Glory: Texts from Gregory of Nyssa's Mystical Writings*, New York: St Vladimir's Seminary Press, 2004.

3 Peter Groves, *Grace: The Free, Unconditional and Limitless Love of God*, London: Canterbury Press, 2012, p. 5.

4 Athanasius, *On the Incarnation*, Crestwood: St Vladimir's Seminary Press, 2011, p. 53.

5 Luke 1.30.

6 Diarmaid MacCulloch, *Silence: A Christian History*, London: Penguin Books, 2014. pp. 26–7.

7 Joseph Ratzinger, *Introduction to Christianity*, San Francisco: Ignatius Press, 2004, p. 135.

8 Gregory Nazianzus, *Festal Orations* (On the Baptism of Christ, Oration 39, 13), trans. Nonna Verna Harrison, New York: St Vladimir's Seminary Press, 2008.

9 Dietrich Bonhoeffer, *God is in the Manger*, Louisville: Westminster John Knox Press, 2010, p. 50.

10 Groves, *Grace*, p. 24.

11 In 2014, Michael Brown's body was left on a Ferguson street for four hours.

12 In 2020, George Floyd had consciousness 'knee'd' out of him by a police officer on camera.

13 In 1993, Stephen Lawrence was murdered at a bus stop in Eltham, London.

14 Bishop Samuel Aziz, *Life and Hope*, Lebanon, 1964, p. 15.

15 www.churchofengland.org/prayer-and-worship/worship-texts-and-resources/common-worship/churchs-year/holy-week-and-easter/holy-communion-order-one#mm049, accessed 4.3.21.

Luke 23.46

tells the tale
of the faultless
fallen.
victim.
the perversion
of the Empire's
relentless force –
of crowds which once
stood in Pilate's Palace
calling, still.
For blood,
by the Poplar
Trees.
Somewhere
Between Jerusalem and
Minnesota Streets
Stands the cross,
hand in hand
with the lynching
tree –
and we who,
washing our hands,
refusing to see ourselves –
are here,
refusing to see –
that Jesus
was George Floyd
killed by the very
same powers –
two thousand
years ago, and –
still.
struggling.
to.
breathe.

'crying out in a loud voice, he breathed his last.'

J. R. B.

3

Grace Crucified

'It is such a mysterious place, the land of tears.'

Antoine de Saint-Exupéry, *The Little Prince*

Ultimately, all Christian reflections on God and the mystery of our faith begin and end with Jesus: his life, his death, his resurrection and ascension. To say this is to say that 'all theological statements win their Christian character only through their connection with Jesus'.[1] And so, as Christians, because the anonymity of God is undone in the work of the incarnation (God becoming flesh) whether we are LGBTQ+ or otherwise, we know God most fully only as God has been revealed in and through Jesus (Colossians 1.15–20). It is essential, then, in our thinking about grace and our Black Queer Christian lives to continue our meditation on the incarnate God in the person of Christ and, in particular, Jesus and what we might call the politics of his cross. If we were to end our meditations just at Christ's birth in Bethlehem we would miss out on all that Jesus in his adult life and experience has to say to us, about us and about our place in this world. Whenever we talk about the gift that is the grace of God, we must never set it apart from the self-offering of Jesus on the cross for us. Connecting the notion of grace to Jesus keeps grace inclusive. To talk about grace in connection to the crucified Jesus is in a sense to limit its interpretation to the cross, and this I think is a good thing. It means that grace cannot be played with into distortion, that its central meaning, its central image, is of the Jesus who gave his life for *all* people. The cross, although at face value both gruesome and brutal, locates grace as pure gift in the body of Jesus, which is torn for the life of the entire world.

As a word, grace finds its root in the Hebrew word *chesed* (*Heh-Sed*). It's not easy to translate into English, but it is vital for our ability to understand God's relationship to us. It is used at least 250 times in the Hebrew Bible (Old Testament) and is often translated as mercy, kindness, goodness, faithfulness and loyalty – yet none of these are quite right.

The closest translation of *chesed* into English is 'loving-kindness'. We see this in various forms particularly in verses such as:

> *In overflowing wrath for a moment I hid my face from you, but with everlasting love [chesed] I will have compassion on you, says the LORD, your Redeemer.*

Isaiah 54.8

> *For the mountains may depart and the hills be removed, but my steadfast love [chesed] shall not depart from you.*

Isaiah 54.10

> *The steadfast love [chesed] of the LORD never ceases, his mercies never come to an end.*

Lamentations 3.22

> *He has told you, O mortal, what is good; and what does the LORD require of you but to do justice, and to love kindness [chesed], and to walk humbly with your God?*

Micah 6.8

> *But I will sing of your might; I will sing aloud of your steadfast love [chesed] in the morning.*

Psalm 59.16

These various examples show that loving-kindness is not only about God's love for us, and God's grace towards us, but also shapes the kind of grace and love that we are to show to one another and to the world. A beautiful example of *chesed* in the New Testament is seen in the story of the good Samaritan. Interestingly, people often forget that when Jesus is asked the questions, 'What must I do to inherit eternal life?' and 'Who is my neighbour?' in Luke 10.25–37, his response is to tell the story of the good Samaritan. It is the story of a man beaten up by robbers, stripped and left for dead. He is passed by a priest, a Levite and a Samaritan. The first two pass him by and carry on their way – finding excuses as to why they cannot help the beaten man – but the Samaritan (the one least expected, the outcast) is the one who comes near to him, sees him, is moved by him, goes to him and bandages his wounds. Not only that, but he puts the beaten man on his animal, takes him to an inn, takes care of him and then takes responsibility for the entire bill for his recovery. At the end of this story, Jesus says: 'Go and do likewise.' In this story, the parable of the good Samaritan, love is the key to salvation – the kind of love that is willing to draw near, to see and to be moved by the 'other'. Many saw the beaten-up man on the road side, but only one was willing to draw near to him and to be moved by what they saw. In one sense we could see the person beaten up by robbers as the Black LGBTQ+ Christian, the priest and Levite as metaphorical representations of the Church and homophobic society. On the other hand, we could also see the Samaritan as an image of the Black LGBTQ+ Christian who, because of their own sense of being an outcast, is moved to compassion because they know what it is to be kicked to the kerb and left for dead. However we read this story in Luke's Gospel, what is clear is that it is a powerful image of the kind of love that grace is. It draws near to us, it sees us, it isn't afraid of our woundedness or the places in which we find ourselves. But even more than that, loving-kindness pays the bill for our healing and wholeness, not in part but in full. And the person who pays that bill in full is God made flesh in Christ who loves our Black Queer lives. It is in this story, applied to us as we are, that we begin to see that 'God is not the problem from which we have to be rescued; [God] is the one who graciously gives [their] all to rescue us. Redemption is [God's] idea, and [God's] greatest gift to us.'[2] Everything that God does for humanity can be seen as loving-kindness – everything that God does in Christ is grace. Grace is the love of God that touches us and draws close to us, not as despised sinners but as those who are accepted, redeemed and already forgiven. It is only an understanding of grace as the loving-kindness of God that offers it to us as the liberating force that it is, as the action of God already at work in our lives, which has been poured out in the hearts of those who follow Christ not just at the point to which they respond but at the point of history in which he offered up his life for the life of the world. As the Methodist Old Testament scholar Professor John N. Oswalt notes:

> The word *hesed* ... [is] the descriptor par excellence of God in the Old Testament. The word speaks of a completely undeserved kindness and generosity done by a person who is in a position of power. This was the Israelites' experience of God. He revealed himself to them when they were not looking for him, and he kept his covenant with them long after their persistent breaking of it had destroyed any reason for his continued keeping of it ... Unlike humans, this deity was not fickle, undependable, self-serving, and grasping. Instead he was faithful, true, upright, and generous – always.[3]

In Psalm 136, the words 'his love endures for ever' are repeated in every verse, and this love is *chesed*. It is out of this love that God creates the world (Genesis 1.1), out of this love that God feeds the hungry (Psalm 145.15), out of this love that God liberates the oppressed (Exodus 14.22), out of this love that God defends the fatherless, the refugee and the widow (Deuteronomy 10.18), out of this love that Christ goes to the cross (Mark 14.36).

Ultimately, the meaning of this Hebrew word is a deep and rich meaning that English simply cannot contain. It is a long-term, lasting, faithful, rock-solid and enduring love – the very kind of love many of us seek to find in human romance, and sometimes find or perhaps still seek. It is the kind of love that exhausts itself in the act of loving – an unswerving loyalty to even the most undeserving and unworthy. The crucified grace of God is a desiring kind of love, which desires us in the totality of our Blackness and our LGBTQ+ identities. It is this love that we can see as characteristic of grace, that we see exampled in the Queer love of David for Jonathan (1 Samuel 18.1–3) and Ruth for Naomi (Ruth 1.16–17), both of which speak of a love that is enduring, gentle and faithful, characterized by a mutual commitment but which we as Black LGBTQ+ Christians may never have seen as similar to our love for one another, and certainly wouldn't have heard in this Queer way in church. The crucified grace of God in Jesus exists to resist the kind of erasure that occurs both in our reading of scripture and within Christian communities. Queer love has been present in many places throughout the history of Jewish and Christian faith, but our heteronormative 'Christian' readings of Queer love as sin has so often meant these Queer dynamics have been left unexplored. Grace exists (because it gives us the confidence that we are loved) to make us more our true selves. When seen in this way, grace is that which should cause a downward move in us (into the truest and deepest parts of our true selves) rather than an upward move in us that takes us out of ourselves – it is the thing that enables us to live completely and fully in our skin with comfort and pride. Grace, the crucified love of God, makes me more comfortable with me. It is that which enables me to see myself as God sees me. If it is about transformation, it is the transformation of my self-image, such that I realize in all that I face – the homophobia, the transphobia, the racism, the misogyny – the loving-kindness of God is unshaken and unchanged, and what reminds me of this is Christ and his cross.

As we meditate on the person of Jesus we begin to see that it is both at the cradle and at the cross – in it and through it – that God shows solidarity not only with the Black and LGBTQ+ people of the world but with the message and praxis of his Son. Jesus speaks to the crucified people of the world, those who know pain and suffering intimately, as one who is himself crucified. In the understanding of many of the earliest theologians, Jesus' humanity was not tied down to his cradle alone – instead it extended far beyond the moment of his birth in Bethlehem and culminates, finds its climax, not in the cradle but at Calvary, on the cross. In being born in Bethlehem as one of us and the child of Mary, Jesus shares in our birth, and in being crucified an enemy of the Empire Jesus shares in our death, suffering and oppression. In life, death and resurrection, Jesus shows the deepest solidarity with humanity.

At the heart of the Christian faith and essential to our understanding of grace is this paradox – not only does God in the birth of Jesus (a little brown Middle-eastern baby) become small and vulnerable, but God in the death of Jesus takes the worst that we can do to him and turns it into the best God can do for us. Our lives in their brokenness, humiliation, pain and suffering become that which is no longer alien to God, but known intimately by God in God's beloved Jesus Christ. In the Christian tradition, Jesus is most human when enthroned in glory upon the cross. It is grace that enables us to believe in the paradox of a wounded Saviour who gives his life for a world made up of many people, including us who are Black and Queer. What we learn in the crucified Jesus is that Jesus speaks his most profound words to the world not with his lips but with his wounds.

Of course, there are many different ways of looking at the wounded Jesus. One of the most fascinating to me is that of the fourteenth-century mystic and hermit Julian of Norwich, who writes in a particularly Queer way about Jesus and his suffering. Locked away from most of the world, Julian receives visions from the Lord that lead to her understanding of who God is. Not only does she believe that God's love is unchanging but she queers Jesus in how she describes him:

> We know that our mothers bear us and bring us into this world to suffering and to death, and yet our true mother Jesus, he, all love, gives birth to us into joy and to endless life – blessed may he be! So he sustains us within himself in love and was in labour for the full time, he who wanted to suffer the sharpest pangs and the most grievous suffering that ever were or ever shall be, and at the last he died. And when he had finished and so given birth to us into bliss, not even all this could satisfy his marvellous love; and he revealed that in these exaltedly surpassing words of love: 'If I could suffer more, I would suffer more.'[4]

For Julian, Jesus is a mother who keeps male pronouns yet who tenderly feeds us with himself, and who leads us intimately into his 'sweet open side' within which we discover not just who God is, but the joys of heaven, spiritual courage and everlasting bliss. It is only Jesus who can inhabit this Queer existence for Julian, because he is the true mother of creation.

Anyone, Julian says, 'who in this life willingly chooses God out of love may be sure of being loved without end, and this endless love works that grace in them'.[5] The crucified grace of God in Jesus communicates to us in how our understandings of God's positionality in the world are queered by the space Jesus himself takes up, and the way his wounds turn his body into a body that is both open to the world and becomes pregnant with the possibility for life pouring from it, through his blood, into the entire world. It is Jesus' deep knowledge of trauma, of pain and suffering that render him a Queer body at the centre of a faith that inflicts trauma, pain and suffering on Queer bodies.

So what can the cross teach us in relation to the cradle? What might the cross say about God's solidarity with lesbian, gay, bisexual, transgender, Queer and non-binary Black folk? Although it is easy to overlook, Jesus is executed by the political and religious powers of his day. It is the collusion of the religious with the secular that leads to the cross. Beyond the sanitized image of Jesus that we have been given, and so inherited, exists a radical charismatic Jewish rabbi who was viewed by the powers of the Roman Empire as the political insurgent that he was. Jesus was a rebel – we might even call him a 'bad-man' – who displayed this side of himself even in his childhood when he disappeared from his parents apparently of his own accord and when found later in the Temple turned to his mother and essentially said, 'Why were you searching for me, didn't you know I'd be here?' Time and again this independent and strong-headed streak in Jesus lands him in trouble. The cross, as an object of cruelty and intimidation, was a political weapon. In the same way in which lynching trees, police uniforms, heteronormativity and Whiteness in general function to keep us who are Black and Queer 'in our place', so too the cross kept those who might upset the principalities and powers of the day in their place. In the same way that Black Queer bodies are deemed deviant for resisting norms and challenging oppressive (often religious and cultural) powers, so too was Jesus' body in the context of an Empire and religious community that did not want him to be free. As a method of control and coercion,

Crucifixion was a Roman form of public service announce-
ment: Do not engage in sedition as this person has, or your
fate will be similar. The point of the exercise was not the
death of the offender as such, but getting the attention of
those watching. Crucifixion first and foremost is addressed
to an audience.[6]

The cross, therefore, is a tool of fear – a fear that those of us
in the Black LGBTQ+ communities know all too well. It is the
kind of fear that prevents us walking too closely to the White
person on the pavement ahead of us who is inconveniently not
just slow but walking in the middle of the pavement. It is the
kind of fear that makes us think twice before we dress ourselves, thinking 'too fem', 'too masc' … 'too Black and angry'.
It is the kind of fear that prevents us participating in the lives
of Christian communities, or answering honestly the 'How's
your love life?' question at family events. It is the kind of fear
that causes us to think through all the consequences that come
with finding love, and making that love public in the world.
Jesus knows what it means to live a life in which your body,
language and freedom exist under the surveillance of powers
that can and do inflict harm. Jesus knew the power of the
White gaze and imperial systemic violence. As the Womanist
and Black Catholic theologian M. Shawn Copeland puts it:

> The supreme Roman penalty, crucifixion was a military and
> political punishment primarily used against insurrectionists,
> murderers, robbers, and reserved in nearly all instances for
> men and women of the lower classes, slaves, and subjugated
> peoples. Crucifixion was intended to intimidate by example
> and subdue by spectacle; it was high state theatrical violence.
> Crucifixion called for the public display of a naked victim in
> some prominent place – at a crossroads, in an amphitheatre,
> on high ground. Often the condemned was flogged, then
> made to carry a crossbeam through the streets to the place of
> execution. The victim's hands and feet were bound or nailed
> to the wood. If, after this torment, the victim were still alive,
> he could expect to die by suffocation: unable to support the
> weight of the body with torn hands, the upper body pressed
> down and slowly crushed the diaphragm.[7]

So, quickly, the connection between the brutal and unjust death that Jesus suffered and the brutal, unjust and public deaths of many Black and Brown lives in today's world becomes clear. Where our bodies stand today, Jesus placed himself 2000 years earlier. In the book of the prophet Isaiah, we hear about one who 'By a perversion of justice was taken away'. Our minds, indeed our hearts, pull up for us not Jesus alone but the murderous deaths of Stephen Lawrence, Michael Menson, Anthony Walker, Sharon Bubb, as well as the deaths of Mark Duggan, Darren Cumberbatch, Rashan Charles, Shane Bryant and Edson da Costa, related to the use of force by the police.[8] These deaths are so often unexplained, always (like every murder of this kind) unwarranted, and motivated by a hatred that too frequently escapes justice. We can think too of the very public deaths in the United States of Eric Garner, Ahmaud Arbery and George Floyd, as well as those not caught on film, of Michael Brown and Breonna Taylor. The list is endless.

Jesus, as a crucified body to crucified bodies, stands as a witness to the fact that institutional brutality, systemic injustice and cultural violence – of the kind that leads to death – is not a myth. That God allows such violence to be borne witness to by Jesus shows just how far God is willing to reach into and inhabit the rough edges of our human reality. Jesus exists in the world as one whom the world touches, and one with whom the world has its way – as it does with us all. It is God in Christ who lives in the world as one who is subject to the same violence, systems of oppression, cruelties and religious hypocrisy that we know and sometimes cannot name. God in Christ is truly human with all that that entails, and truly divine in what he does with that humanity – and that in itself is grace.

The violence and politics of the cross reaches into our experience not just as Black Christians but as Black LGBTQ+ Christians too. Robert Goss captures this perfectly in his challenging of the abusive uses of Jesus' suffering. Although speaking particularly of the oppression of gay and lesbian people, his words are true for LGBTQ+ people more widely:

> The cross symbolizes the political infrastructure of homophobic practice and oppression. It symbolizes the terror

of internalized homophobia that has led to the closeted invisibility of gay and lesbian people. It indicates the brutal silencing, the hate crimes, the systemic violence perpetuated against us. The cross now belongs to us. We have been crucified.[9]

For Goss, the death of Jesus 'shapes the cross into a symbol of struggle for queer liberation'.[10] In being nailed to the cross, Jesus identifies with all those who experience a pain and carry a burden that is inflicted and laid upon them – not because of anything they have done, but because of who they are. Jesus is nailed to the cross because of his identity as the Son of God (a claim that was blasphemous) as much as for his preaching, teaching and radical love in an Empire that did not want him to be true to his calling and identity. Having come out in the incarnation, Jesus seeking to transgress the binary of life and death finds hatred, mockery and disbelief when his identity as the risen one having come out of the tomb is revealed. In life and in death Jesus could not breathe. Like Eric Garner and George Floyd, under the weight of the knee of the Empire, all that Jesus does is done under the surveillance of imperial powers. Like Stephen Lawrence and Breonna Taylor, Jesus existed as one perceived as a threat not just while on the streets but even while he slept. He who on the cross screamed out his soul into the hands of his Father, and 'Having said this, he breathed his last' (Luke 23.46), knew the fragility of Black life. It is as one of us that Jesus breathes his last with all those who have the life of God snuffed out of them by the violent forces of this world. Jesus breathes his last with those murdered as sex workers. Jesus breathes his last with the young Black LGBTQ+ human being who has deemed life not worth living having looked out into the future and seen nothing but despair. Jesus breathes his last with all of us in a world rife with homophobic, trans-phobic and racist social sin. In the economy of God's grace, we take neither our first breath nor our last breath alone – both, because of the cradle and the cross, are taken with a wounded yet risen Christ. As Kelly Brown Douglas says:

[Jesus'] birth in a manger convinced me that he understood the struggles, if not the hopes and dreams, of Black children who were trapped in 'manger-like' conditions of living ... Christ's Blackness indicates his deep and personal identification with people of colour as they suffer the pain, heartache, and death exacted on them by the insidiousness of white Supremacist culture.[11]

In the incarnation, God's life is handed into the hands of humankind in a way that leads to life for all, and in the crucifixion God puts Godself into the hands of humanity, which this time means a certain and brutal death. Jesus experiences an execution in which the trial is unjust, the evidence is false and the verdict predetermined. The cross then represents a real revolution, not in God's posture towards the world but in our posture towards God and how we are able to understand that posture – we see now that it is true: 'in Christ God was reconciling the world to himself' (2 Corinthians 5.19) and this is a reconciliation that reaches beyond the moment of Christ's death, into all of time. The wounds of Jesus now speak to us. They speak to us of both the grace and humanity of a God who shows us in Christ's body just how far love will go in search of us, showing us the extent of God's love, a love that enters the world and leads Christ to his death, a love that leads to the Son of God with his arms outstretched in embrace of the world upon the cross.

Heterosexual privilege within the Church has meant that most of us come to understand Jesus by those who have a dominance within our religious and cultural communities. Not only does this dominance silence Queer voices, but it means that any exploration around what Jesus' life, death and resurrection might mean uniquely for the LGBTQ+ community is an exploration that to hetereosexual Christians feels like deliberately disruptive exploration. The Church's authority over Christian theology for centuries has meant that 'it has exercised its authority in a terroristic fashion to silence critics from speaking and exclude them from teaching'.[12] The practice of Queer Christian theologians necessarily pushes back therefore on institutional domination by the Church, and Black Queer theologians on the dominance of Whiteness on theology more generally. The perception over the many years of Christianity's dominating presence of a God who is both White and male has been a key component to the thriving patriarchy, misogynoir and White Supremacy that we see today.

In 2018, Naomi Hersi, a trans woman of colour, was murdered by a White man who stabbed her to death in a hotel having agreed to meet up with her on a website.[13] Her father described what happened as the 'ultimate injustice', and when finally able to share his grief said, 'Our lives will never be the same. The grief has swallowed us up. It's consumed us. Maybe one day it will not be so painful but the violence of [the] death haunts us.' In that very year, the year of Naomi's murder, two in five trans people had experienced a hate crime related to gender identity. One in eight had been physically attacked by a colleague or customer. Four in five do not report hate crimes to the police out of fear of further discrimination. Further to this, one in four trans people have experienced homelessness in their lives, and three in ten non-binary people have experienced a hate crime or incident related to their gender identity.[14] Behind each of these statistics are people for whom Christ gave his life. Behind each story, each scar and wound are individuals loved and cherished by God. While it is popular in many Christian circles to mark the Transgender Day of Remembrance on 20 November each year, we must also question why it is that we are so eager to mark the deaths of trans folk when we do so little to nurture, embrace and protect them while they are alive. The wounded body of Christ is wounded in solidarity with a broken world. It is wounded with all those whose identity has cost them their lives. It is not good enough for the Body of Christ to openly remember trans folk who are dead, when we have not vocally, physically and theologically done all we can to protect, nurture and affirm them when they are with us in body. If death is the motivation for our solidarity with the suffering, then we have misunderstood the gospel, misunderstood Christ's cross, misunderstood the meaning of Christianity. If we cannot see Christ in the Black trans community, if we cannot see Christ suffering among them and in them, then we have both an image of Christ and an image of our trans siblings that denies the image of God in both. Perhaps it is all too easy to ignore the similarities between Christ and the trans experience of transitioning. Christ in his birth is not recognized as who he will one day become – who he truly is. There are three people, wise magi from the East, who seem to know and understand that a King has been born, and who act upon that knowledge. Yet, Christ is revealed as his full self only when he has five wounds that make him who he really is. It is the wounds he bears, the scars upon his body, and the stories those scars tell, that reveal him post his transition on the cross to be the Saviour. The wounds that Jesus carries are those that make him who he is, and that render him recognizable to us in his fullest and truest identity not as a carpenter from Nazareth but as the one through whom our salvation comes, as the one who is truly seen – having passed through death – as the Son of God. When Jesus is crucified and almost dead – named by the notice above him 'King of the Jews' – he shares in the experience of being mocked, ridiculed and misidentified that so many in the trans and non-binary communities know. Jesus' solidarity with us knows no bounds. Speaking of the way in which W. E. B. Du Bois entered into the Black experience of life for Black folk in the diaspora, C. Riley Snorton notes that to feel Black in the diaspora might be to enter into something of the trans experience in which one knows the 'peculiar sensation' of 'always looking at one's self through the eyes of others, of measuring one's soul by the tape of a world that looks on in amused contempt and pity'.[15]

When scripture tells us that Jesus 'was in the world, and the world came into being through him; yet the world did not know him. He came to what was his own, and his own people did not accept him' (John 1.10–11), it is hard not to identify with this sense of peculiar sensation that Jesus must have felt in a world that had so much contempt for him and his identity. We must be cautious when thinking about Jesus' crucifixion, however, not to romanticize it. Jesus' death was a real death. Although we might have a hard time truly understanding how it is that the Son of God could fully die and know the fullness of that death, a death that is ours, to view his death in any other way is to minimize its power. Jesus knew the depths of our despair in the pain of the cross. We must resist any temptation 'to imagine him waking up in heaven from a momentary slumber, the mortal life a bad dream, the phase of his humanity over and done'.[16] For Jesus this experience of death is total, not just partial. With Naomi Hersi, Mark Duggan, Breonna Taylor and George Floyd, Jesus enters the darkness of the grave – and like their parents weeping at the sites of the death and at the news of it, so Mary weeps at the foot of the cross. A Black mother weeping for the death of her Black child, like so many who come after her. Jesus' friends know the helplessness that comes from a death brought about through sheer injustice, the powerlessness of losing in what seems like the face of a relentless and brutal law enforcement. Jesus' death was Black in its experience because Jesus died like so many Black and Brown people today, and his death is Queer in its ending in both a lack of justice and resurrection. God comes as flesh in Christ that is not only born but buried. God comes as flesh in Christ that not only brings healing but is brutalized. God comes as flesh that is not only loved but is hated – God's relationship with our life is Queer and unstable. What is turned upside down between God's coming to humanity as flesh in the birth of Jesus in Bethlehem and God crucified in Jesus at Calvary is not God but rather our ideas of God. Between the cradle, the cross and the resurrection all of our ideas about God – who God is, who God isn't, what God can and cannot do – are flipped. Our minds must stretch to comprehend a Creator who is wounded in the flesh of the Son, a Son who remains with us in his Spirit. It is a Queer thing that the divine love of God suffers and dies for creation. It is a Queer thing that God comes to us in a baby. It is a Queer thing that God's method of salvation should function in such a way that the Creator stoops down to us rather than summons us to the lofty heights of heaven. It is perhaps for this reason that St Paul in the letter to the church in Ephesus says: 'I pray that you may have the power to comprehend, with all the saints, what is the breadth and length and height and depth, and to know the love of Christ that surpasses knowledge' (Ephesians 3.18–19). Dr Martin Luther King Jr, on the cross and the love of God, says:

The greatest of all virtues is love. Here we find the true meaning of the Christian faith and of the cross. Calvary is a telescope through which we look into the loving vista of eternity and see the love of God breaking into time. Out of the hugeness of his generosity God allowed his only-begotten Son to die that we may live. By uniting yourselves with Christ and your brothers through love you will be able to matriculate in the university of eternal life. In a world depending on force, coercive tyranny, and bloody violence, you are challenged to follow the way of love. You will then discover that unarmed love is the most powerful force in all the world.[17]

The remembrance of a wounded Jesus has been central to so many theologies of liberation around the world. In particular, the idea of a 'crucified people' has been foundational to the theology of Catholic priest and liberation theologian Jon Sobrino. Not only does Sobrino see what he calls the 'crucified people' as making Christ present in the world by bearing so evidently the cross, but 'they also make him present because, like the lamb of God, they carry the sin of the world and by carrying it offer light and salvation to all'.[18] There is something both beautiful and deeply challenging in Sobrino's understanding of the suffering as a 'crucified people', but most profound is his associating the suffering people with Christ. For Sobrino, 'the present day crucified people allow us to know the crucified Christ better'.[19] In Sobrino's understanding, those who die among the crucified peoples die a distinctly inflicted death, a death that is so recognizably a 'Black death'. 'To die crucified does not mean simply to die, but to be put to death; it means that there are victims and there are executioners.'[20] This language of crucified peoples enables us to see those who are oppressed within and beyond the Church as Jesus Christ.

It is useful and necessary language at the religious level because cross – Jesus suffered death on the cross and not any other death – evokes sin and grace, condemnation and salvation, human action and God's action. From a Christian point of view, God himself makes himself present in these crosses, and the crucified peoples become the principal sign of the times.[21]

In this way, those who are Black and LGBTQ+, who know the suffering of exclusion, discrimination or the very real suffering of physical violence, are a sign of the suffering Christ in the world. We act as a mirror to the times in a world and a church that has once again found it necessary to crucify the innocent. Those who are among the crucified peoples bear witness too to the solidarity that human beings find in suffering. As Black LGBTQ+ Christians find each other, and refuse to let one another go, we bear witness to the love of Christ that cannot be contained in any system or institution – we live as the crucified among Christ who are sometimes abandoned in an extra-ecclesial exile.

Jesus, in dying the way he dies, models the self-emptying love of God that is necessary in the Church today if the crucified peoples are ever to be acknowledged. Jesus models what theologians call 'kenosis' – the self-emptying of Jesus' own will in response to the will of his Father.

> *Let the same mind be in you that was in Christ Jesus,*
> *who, though he was in the form of God,*
> *did not regard equality with God*
> *as something to be exploited,*
> *but emptied himself,*
> *taking the form of a slave,*
> *being born in human likeness.*
> *And being found in human form,*
> *he humbled himself*
> *and became obedient to the point of death –*
> *even death on a cross.*

Philippians 2.5–8

What is most inconceivable about Christ's death is that it is a death that expresses itself as a love that asks for nothing in return. This self-emptying of Jesus summons us not only into a deeper discipleship as individuals, but it calls for us to make a similar commitment of solidarity with all those who find themselves to have been by force sent to the edges of the Church and the world. It is of himself that Jesus speaks when he says that 'unless a grain of wheat falls into the earth and dies, it remains just a single grain; but if it dies, it bears much fruit' (John 12.24). If 'The cross [is] an ultimate point of illumination on the character of [humanity] and God',[22] then in looking at the cross we must resist all temptations to try to sugar coat the very gruesome death of Jesus. Death for Jesus is not just partial; the death of the incarnate God is real. If we are honest, we do have a difficulty in really believing that Jesus died in the deepest sense. We find it hard to believe that Jesus truly felt all that death can feel like; we struggle to accept that he knew the deepest depths of hopelessness, betrayal and despair. When we gaze upon the cross, we should recognize that 'God was not only incarnate but interred'.[23] The world is redeemed and reconciled not just through the shedding of Christ's blood without which there could be no remission of sin, but also through his total, complete and entire identification with suffering, dead and dying people. 'It is in our deepest experiences of human love, wrested to extremes and beyond all calculation, that we are first drawn into the meaning of the Passion.'[24]

Christ's solidarity with us is witnessed in his entire life and Jesus defines his ministry, sets the scene for his life and purposes among us on earth in Luke's Gospel when reading from the prophet Isaiah. He says in a synagogue in Nazareth:

'The Spirit of the Lord is upon me,
    because he has anointed me
        to bring good news to the poor.
He has sent me to proclaim release to the captives
    and recovery of sight to the bind,
        to let the oppressed go free,
    to proclaim the year of the Lord's favour.'

Luke 4.18–19

Having done this, he immediately hands the scroll back and sits down. With the eyes of everyone in the synagogue upon him, Jesus turns to them and says, 'Today this scripture has been

fulfilled in your hearing.' In many ways, it is an odd encounter.
Jesus being in the synagogue is no strange thing. Jesus himself
being Jewish and this being the Sabbath, where else should
he have been? What is important is that Jesus tells the people
in the synagogue that the words they have heard from the
prophet of the past have been fulfilled in their present. It is as
though Jesus, in his very reading of those words, aligns himself
not only with the prophetic tradition but with the words themselves. Jesus is making a claim, in what is often referred to as
the 'Nazareth Manifesto', to what he sees as his mission, his
vision for the world, his Kingdom policies. Good news not to
the rich but to the poor, release to the captive, recovery of sight
to those who do not see, freedom for the oppressed ... words
that Jesus' mother Mary would not have been opposed to, as
earlier in the same Gospel, having heard that she would bring
this Jesus into the world, Mary who was rad and eloquently
Black sings:

> 'My soul magnifies the Lord,
>   and my spirit rejoices in God my Saviour,
> for he has looked with favour on the lowliness of his servant.
>   Surely, from now on all generations will call me blessed;
> for the Mighty One has done great things for me,
>   and holy is his name.
> His mercy is for those who fear him
>   from generation to generation.
> He has shown the strength with his arm;
>   he has scattered the proud in the thoughts of their hearts.
> He has brought down the powerful from their thrones,
>   and lifted up the lowly;
> he has filled the hungry with good things,
>   and sent the rich away empty.
> He has helped his servant Israel,
>   in remembrance of his mercy,
> according to the promise he made to our ancestors,
>   to Abraham and to his descendants for ever.'

Luke 1.46–55

In Jesus' words in the synagogue and Mary's song of praise we see a mother and son who together have a view of a world where justice reigns and power is controlled and shared. It is an image of a world that sits so contrary to much of the Christianity we often see. What it teaches us is a different way of being, where goodness and freedom are the marks of life in God. As Peter Rollins says so clearly:

> I deny the resurrection of Christ every time I do not serve at the feet of the oppressed, each day that I turn my back on the poor … when I close my ears to the cries of the downtrodden and lend my support to an unjust and corrupt system.

All Christians who are content with LGBTQ+ exclusion deny what they proclaim by the way they live, and only those Christians who benefit from systems of oppression can sustain a relationship with a Jesus who is politically neutral in the face of injustice.

One of the problems with White gay men existing at the hegemonic centre of the Queer community is that our Black LGBTQ+ experience is elided. This erasure, experienced not just in real life but even via social media, when combined with Black homophobia, adds to further this. The fact is that as well as being erased in our Blackness by the LGBTQ+ communities, within the Black community there are those who look like us and love like us but do not stand with us, and a number of people who consider themselves our allies but only show a secret solidarity. Of course, Black allies within the Church who are not vocal do not seriously want Black LGBTQ+ people to breathe; if they did, they would speak up. All of this can so often leave us with the sense and struggle of existing as divided souls, misunderstood in a world where nowhere feels accepting. As Black LGBTQ+ people living under the multiple marginalizations that brings, this feeling of nowhere accepting us can be a factor in the extent to which we go out into the world in search of love or inclusion. This searching though, Essex Hemphill notes, can sometimes – especially in those who lack a grammar of suffering – mean that although we end up in dangerous places in the name of love or desire, those places can prepare us for the radical social action society so desperately needs. In the book quoting Hemphill, Darius Bost writes:

> Even though the dangers of public sex might have prepared Black gay men for the possible physical dangers of activism in hostile environments, the multiple fronts on which these men were fighting for racial and sexual freedom must have taken a psychic toll.[25]

Our exclusion from the Church as part of this also pushes us towards the activism and social work that the Church itself should be doing, yet on the other hand it can also lead to us seeking intimacy in ways that feed our skin hunger but not necessarily our heartfelt longing. As Melvin Dixon describes ultimately as the hardness of being gay in one of his diary entries:

> I don't feel sexual, just [need] someone to talk to. My utmost desire is to be held. Not fucked, sucked or cruised. Just gently, and affectionately held, embraced. Covered with fire from someone's hot flesh – who wants me, needs me – not so much sexually, but humanly, tenderly, soft but firm. How tired I am of the 'hardness' of being gay.[26]

In expressing the search for somewhere to belong, Alexander Leon, a writer and campaigner for LGBT+ rights based in the UK, articulated how the hypersexuality he experienced as a young gay man pressed incessantly upon him and felt like the only way for him to find belonging. Movingly he said: 'I wanted mentors. I got darkrooms.' In a world where he was confronted by what he experienced as an unforgiving social scene as a young gay man, he remarked: 'We seek spiritual guidance in our sexual conquests and come up short time and time again.'[27] Alexander notes that for those whose bodies do not quite fit in, theirs was a dwindling currency in a context where being a certain type of sexual body led to acceptance or rejection. People, he says, 'deserve spaces where they are taught that by virtue of being gay, they already belong and have value'.[28] In an extended essay on the same theme, he describes how that journey into authentic living as LGBTQ+ people takes work, including spiritual work:

This task, of finding ourselves, is a massive, existential and deeply difficult exercise that all queer people share but seldom collectively acknowledge. It's a task that leads many of us down treacherous paths, chasing other forms of escapism that mirror the closet, drinking or drugging ourselves into other forms of suspended reality where we can pretend again. It's a task that involves enormous emotional and spiritual upheaval, which many of us are forced to do alone, with scant resources, or little in the form of mentorship.[29]

Although Alexander Leon doesn't cite Christian faith as part of his experience, for many in the process of coming out the one source of spiritual solace and support is swiftly pulled away. As we grow into our authentic selves we find that the Christian community either retreats from us or sends us into exile.

This is movingly articulated in Mr Ekow's story 'No Man's Land'. Ekow grew up in South London and identifies as a British Ghanaian, gay, Christian. In his own words he retells his story of coming out in his context as someone brought up in the Church and for whom Christianity was his identity. Moving from a Baptist context to the Charismatic tradition he recalls how he witnessed God at work and how at a young age he committed his life to God. He describes something common to many Black contexts, the absence of ever questioning the reality of God among his friends, but rather asking: 'How real do you want to take this?' The challenge came, though, when he began to wrestle with his sexuality in the midst of Christian community. Although he never experienced being forced to 'pray the gay away', he did seek guidance from the leaders around him and from other church members, and began to position his sexuality as a thing of the past. While this experience took him further away from his Christian kin, it took him closer to God.

> I would cry with him (or her), get angry with him (or her) …
> I spent a lot of time praying. Looking back now, a lot of it
> was genuine – I felt closer to God and gained a deeper understanding of the scripture – but it was coated with rejection.[30]

After a number of failed attempts in heterosexual relation-ships, and only being met with offers of prayer from other Christians, the 'narrative of reject, reject, reject, continued' for Ekow.[31] Both therapy and a drunken night gave Ekow the clarity to realize that he had to come out. At first he came out to just a few friends, then plucked up the courage to tell his parents. His dad wasn't particularly bothered and said that people should do what they want to do, his mother though was upset but eventually came around. The question remained: could he be gay and Christian at the same time? It was finding Oasis Church in London, receiving therapy and reworking his theology that helped Ekow.

> My Christianity has changed, my faith is a lot simpler, but I am happy. I am trying to love God as much as I can, love others as much as I can, and move forward. It's working for me. I am at the point where I think God loves gay people. And this isn't to say, God loves gay people, but he hates their sin'. God loves gay people. I have a partner now, and we often talk about religion. He wasn't raised with faith, so we can have conversations that are free of all the politics. We educated each other and question each other.[32]

Of course many of us do not have Mr Ekow's experience, either with the Church or with our families, and it is harrow-ing to call to mind that not only are LGBTQ+ people twice as likely to consider suicide[33] than non-LGBTQ+ people but one in seven trans people have been offered services to stop them being trans,[34] and many trans people are also LGB. For many of us who come out in the midst of Christian commu-nities that are not affirming, our experience of rejection can be lethal. The prevalence of this rejection, coupled with 'con-version therapy', can mean that many of us who come out, or think about doing so, do not survive the experience. The affect that bad theology and harmful spiritual practices have on our physical and mental health cannot be overlooked, and every act of harm committed in this way is a denial of the grace and love of God. It is an indictment of our life together that 'con-version therapy' has not been banned in the UK despite it being such an abhorrent practice. Essential work to ban this abusive torture 'treatment' is being done by Matthew Hyndman and Harry Hitchens through the organization Ban Conversion Therapy,[35] but despite two recent prime ministers vowing to ban it this still has not happened.[36] Faith organizations, healthcare providers and family members are the avenues through which people receive this awful treatment and it is hard to imagine a great chasm between the teaching of the Church and those faith organizations and religious families.

Father Jide Macaulay, my friend and colleague, has been instrumental in countering some of the negative and harmful understandings of Black LGBTQ+ existence not just in the UK but around the world, particularly in Nigeria and other parts of Africa. Jide founded the House of Rainbow as an organization that enables the fostering of relationships and the creating of safer communities for Black, Asian Minority Ethnic and LGBTQ+ individuals and allies. As an openly gay Anglican priest and HIV+ activist, Jide has tirelessly laboured to provide inclusive biblical teaching, mentoring to those with HIV, support for LGBTQ+ asylum seekers, and pastoral care to those of us whom the 'mainstream' Church has largely forgotten. Although churches such as the Metropolitan Community Church (MCC) and the Inclusive Church network exist, they are largely places centred on White Christian worship styles, where someone who is politically Black, or seeking inclusive charismatic African worship for example, might not feel at home. What we are reminded of in the ministry of remarkably courageous individuals like Jide and others is that love, if it is driven by grace, always leads us to seek out those who are beyond the Church's walls. As well as our actions in this sense, our theological work is equally important in terms of what we write, say and preach. Those of us who exist within the established structures of the Church often pay a high price for our honesty and openness, yet there may be a deeper boldness needed if we are to disrupt, deconstruct and stand against all that stands contrary in the Church's teaching to the thriving of Black LGBTQ+ life. Gesturing powerfully towards this, Pamela Lightsey says that Black theologians, particularly those writing from within the academy and as Christian clergy, really need to be bolder and say categorically that human sexuality expressed consensually in loving acts, including intercourse, is not sin. She writes challengingly:

> LGBTQ persons should ignore Church teaching against consensual sex as an expression of love between same-sex persons. They should derive every possible pleasure from engaging in it and understand it as a healthy expression of what it means to be human. Without this affirmation and scholarly assessment of impractical and poor church theology, we have few resources that will help us be whole persons within the churches we adore.[37]

One of the difficulties of growing up in a church that is homophobic is that Christianity is both theological formation and sex education. By this I mean that those of us who have lived all our lives within the Christian community have had our theology and our sexual ethics shaped by the teaching of the Church. The work of undoing when it comes to this, even for those of us who are Black clergy and theologians, is a lifelong task – the summons from Lightsey is an important one and one that must be heard, notwithstanding its challenge.

In coming into our world as one of us, and physically embodying the grace of God, Jesus shows us who God is and what God is like. If we want to know what God is like, we have to look at Jesus. In looking at him, we see one who is more at home in the company of tax collectors and sinners than he is in the company of sages and saints. Jesus has a love for the outcast, for those whom society has rejected, overlooked and persecuted. What we also see and come to recognize in Jesus is that God's love for us – for the world – is not transactional. God's love is a promiscuous love, a radical love, an abundant love.

In the fourth chapter of John's Gospel Jesus causes a bit of a stir among the disciples. On his way back to Galilee, he stops in a Samaritan city called Sychar to get some water from Jacob's well. Worn out, thirsty and exhausted by his long journey, Jesus sits down at the well in the excruciating midday heat and suddenly finds himself in the presence of a woman.

In this particular context Jesus, a Jew, was not supposed to interact with Samaritans, let alone a Samaritan woman, but he does. He asks the woman for a drink, and, shocked at his request, she wonders how such a thing could be possible. After pointing out to him that not only is the well very deep but that Jesus appears to have no bucket with him to collect water, she wonders who this man is. Suddenly the story moves in an interesting direction as Jesus begins to talk to her about 'living water' – not like that in the well, which, when people drink it, doesn't satisfy their thirst once and for all, the living water that Jesus gives means that those who drink it 'will never be thirsty' (John 4.13). Like any of us, on hearing of this water the woman says to Jesus, 'Sir, give me this water, so that I may never be thirsty or have to keep coming here to draw water'. Then Jesus says, 'Go, call your husband, and come back.' What transpires is that the woman has no husband, and Jesus appears to know this and knows too that she has had five and the man she is currently with now is not her husband. Rather than deny what Jesus appears to already know about her, she calls him a prophet and engages in a dialogue with Jesus about the Messiah who is to come, and how he will be worshipped and where he will be praised. She tells him of the Messiah about whom she has already heard, one who will 'proclaim all things to us'. And there and then, at the very end of their conversation, Jesus says 'I am he, the one who is speaking to you.'

The telling thing about the interaction between Jesus and the Samaritan woman is how uninterested Jesus seems in the small detail of her situation. He doesn't dig for more details, he isn't interested in why she's had five husbands, he doesn't condemn her or shame her – he sees her as a human being who is, for whatever reason, in a complicated situation, in what some might call an 'entanglement'.[38] So transformative was this encounter that after this the woman drops her water-jar and runs throughout the nearby city telling people about the man she has just met! This is what happens when Jesus, the joy of God, meets us where we are. When his wounds touch our shadow-places, when his tenderness meets us in the closets of our lives, when his love enfolds the parts of us we hide, we come to know the joy that Jesus brings.

As a theologian rooted in a myriad of contexts and situated at multiple sites of oppression, I am not prepared or able to speak and think about grace only in relation to notions of brokenness and sin. The Queer theologian Patrick S. Cheng considers grace as the companion doctrine of sin. Ultimately, he believes that it is time now for LGBT people to take back the words 'sin' and 'grace' in the same way that the LGBTQ+ communities have taken back the word 'Queer'. My contention (and it may be an unfair contention) with this position is not that these words cannot be redeemed, but that we, the Church, must allow grace to speak for itself. Cheng sees grace as an amazing gift from God that helps us to be reunited with God after a period of separation.[39] My disagreement with notions such as this are that they cannot but feed the sense that separation from God is a real possibility in this life, and that grace can only repair rather than enhance our relationship with God. That said, Cheng holds a challenging perspective as simultaneously grace for Cheng is 'obscenely promiscuous'.[40]

If grace requires a nearer following of Christ to be truly effective then many heterosexual Christians have yet to model such discipleship for the LGBTQ+ community. It seems so often an act of violence rooted in a deep theological rupture that the multiple demands that grace apparently makes upon humankind fall upon the Queer community delivered by heterosexual hands. And, if grace is fundamentally about us no longer being who we once were, if grace is about a transformation that demands the costly transformation that renders us incomplete, if grace is understood as making the LGBTQ+ 'straight' and eradicating our 'Blackness', then it is not of God and is a threat to the freedom of the LGBTQ+ community of every hue, who are the beloved children of God. The late Archbishop of Canterbury, Michael Ramsey, wrote:

> Like the Christ, the Church is sent to execute a twofold work in the face of the sufferings of [all]; to seek to alleviate them, to heal them and to remove them, since they are hateful to God – yet, when they are overwhelming and there is no escape from them, to transfigure them and use them as the raw material of love. So in every age Christians have sought

to remove sufferings, and have also borne witness to the truth that they can be transfigured and can become the place where the power of God is known, the Church is a scene of continual dying; yet it is the place where the sovereignty of God is known and uttered, and where God is reconciling the world to Himself. Here life is given in abundance, and here the faithful discern the peace of the resurrection.[41]

Any of us who read Ramsey's words know that both in history and in present fact Christians have indeed sought but rarely succeeded in being the kinds of people Ramsey speaks of. That said, there is something quite profound in his image of the Church as the body that has a mandate to alleviate suffering, where life is given in abundance and where the faithful (all God's gathered people) come to know the peace of Christ crucified, risen and ascended. Despite this, the charge made of inclusive churches is often that they have abandoned their mandate to be faithful to scripture and have made God's grace cheap – offering it without the demands that the gospel apparently clearly requires. Yet it would be truer to charge conservative Christianity with making grace cheap. Homophobic Christianity is rooted in the self-assurance that one can carry the name of Christ and choose when to see that image reflected in one's neighbour. Homophobic Christianity has postured itself as the depository of truth. Homophobic Christianity is the embodiment of cheap grace, the abuse of God's mercy and the denial of the promises of God as it makes a mockery of the very kind of transformation that it demands to see in the life of LGBTQ+ Christians, society and all those who affirm us. Cheng remarks:

> For those of us who walk the Christian path, grace is not just an external 'thing' that we receive from God for spiritual regeneration or growth (for example, a sacrament such as Baptism or the Holy Eucharist), but rather grace is Jesus Christ himself. Jesus Christ, as the Word made flesh, is the ultimate unmerited gift to us from God.[42]

If Jesus Christ himself is grace, if Jesus Christ himself is the ultimate unmerited gift from God to us, then he is not only given to God's people freely but he has already done so in his life, death and resurrection. The cross and resurrection make Jesus' gift of himself to us a fact of history that is not open to change, challenge or diminishment by conservative Christian opinion. In his death and resurrection, Jesus says to the Black LGBTQ+ community, and to the whole world:

I love you.
I am yours.
You are mine.
All this for you, before you could know anything of it.[43]

Notes

1 Wolfart Pannenberg, *Jesus: God and Man*, Philadelphia: Westminster Press, 1964, p. 19.

2 Trevor Hart, in Colin E. Gunton (ed.), *The Cambridge Companion to Christian Doctrine*, Cambridge: Cambridge University Press, 1997, pp. 195–6.

3 John N. Oswalt, *The Bible among the Myths: Unique Revelation or Just Ancient Literature?*, Michigan: Zondervan, 2009.

4 Julian of Norwich, *Revelations of Divine Love*, Oxford: Oxford University Press, 2015, p. 130.

5 Ibid., p. 138.

6 Paula Frederickson, *Jesus of Nazareth, King of the Jews: A Jewish Life and the Emergence of Christianity*, New York: Vintage, 2000, pp. 233–4.

7 M. Shawn Copeland, *Knowing Christ Crucified: The Witness of African American Religious Experience*, New York: Orbis Books, 2018, p. 115.

8 www.theguardian.com/uk-news/2017/sep/03/four-black-men-die-police-restraint-no-officers-suspended-bryant-cumberbatch-charles-da-costa, accessed 18.3.21.

9 Robert Goss, *Jesus Acted Up: A Gay and Lesbian Manifesto*, San Francisco: HarperCollins, 1993, p. 83.

10 Ibid.

11 Kelly Brown Douglas, *The Black Christ*, New York: Orbis Books, 2019, pp. xx–xxi.

12 Goss, *Jesus Acted Up*, p. 63.

13 www.bbc.co.uk/news/uk-england-london-46061200, accessed 18.3.21.

14 www.stonewall.org.uk/cy/node/65106, accessed 18.3.21.

15 C. Riley Snorton, *Black on Both Sides: A Racial History of Trans Identity*, Minneapolis: University of Minnesota Press, 2017, p. 8.

16 Michael Downey, *The Depths of God's Reach*, New York: Orbis Books, 2018, p. 46.

17 Martin Luther King Jr, *A Gift of Love: Sermons from Strength to Love*, London: Penguin Books, 2012, p. 148.

18 Jon Sobrino, *Spiritual Writings*, New York: Orbis Books, 2018, p. 79.

19 Ibid.

20 Ibid., p. 83.

21 Ibid.

22 Reinhold Niebuhr, 'The Power and Weakness of God', in *Discerning the Signs of the Times: Sermons for Today and Tomorrow*, New York: Charles Scribner's Sons, 1946, pp. 140–2.

23 Downey, *The Depths of God's Reach*, p. 50.

24 Sarah Coakley, *The Cross and the Transformation of Desire*, Cambridge: Grove Books, 2014, p. 7.

25 Darius Bost, *Evidence of Being: The Black Gay Cultural Renaissance and the Politics of Violence*, Chicago and London: University of Chicago Press, 2019, p. 50.

26 Melvin Dixon, diary entry, 6 November 1973, box 1, journal folder 22 July 1973–2 May 1974, Melvin Dixon Addition, Schomburg Center for Research in Black Culture, New York Public Library.

27 https://twitter.com/alexand_erleon/status/1207601010731995136, accessed 6.4.21.

28 Ibid.

29 https://medium.com/@alxndrleon/out-of-the-closet-and-into-the-fire-how-i-stopped-performing-and-learned-to-become-myself-6ffodca4463d, accessed 18.3.21.

30 Mr Ekow, in Séan Richardson (ed.), *Unorthodox: LGBT+ Identity and Faith*, Nottingham: Five Leaves Publications, 2019, p. 68.

31 Ibid., p. 69.

32 Ibid., p. 71.

33 https://youth.gov/youth-topics/lgbtq-youth/health-depression-and-suicide, accessed 18.3.21.

34 https://assets.publishing.service.gov.uk/government/uploads/system/uploads/attachment_data/file/722314/GEO-LGBT-Survey-Report.pdf, accessed 4.3.21.

35 www.banconversiontherapy.com/about, accessed 18.3.21.

36 www.bbc.co.uk/news/uk-politics-53477323, accessed 18.3.21.

37 Pamela Lightsey, *Our Lives Matter: A Womanist Queer Theology*, Oregon: Pickwick Publications, 2015, p. 11.

38 www.theguardian.com/tv-and-radio/2020/jul/16/will-smith-jada-pinkett-smith-entanglement-red-table-talks-reality-checked, accessed 18.3.21.

39 Patrick S. Cheng, *From Sin to Amazing Grace: Discovering the Queer Christ*, New York: Seabury Press, p. 24.

40 Ibid., p. 26.

41 Michael Ramsey, *The Gospel and the Catholic Church*, Massachusetts: Cowley Publications, 1990, p. 41.

42 Cheng, *From Sin to Amazing Grace*, p. 30.

43 'All this for you before you could know anything of it' are words spoken in the Methodist liturgy for the Baptism of Young Children.

Monochrome

You say you're 'colour-blind'
if so – you can't see me.
I am a million shackled rainbows
hidden from a child's view.
I am the strange fruit that fed you.
I am the sun drained
of its golden hue.
I am the caged bird
without a note to sing.
I am the dream you li(v)e in.
You say you're 'colour-blind'
if so – you can't see me.
I am the smile your
blindness forces me behind.
I am your lie.
I am your tithe.
I am your wife for a night and nine months.
I am a million dreams cut short.
I am the Golliwog you taught to talk.
You say you're 'colour-blind'
if so – you can't see me.
I, am a Mandela waiting for release.
I, am a Martin killed by peace.
I, am a Malcolm shot dead by police.
I, am a Harriet still setting free.
I, am Muhammad stinging like a bee.
I am these and these are me, and we are legion.
The negroes you never shackled
to be free.

J. R. B.

4

Grace and Queer Black Bodies

You got to love it. This is flesh I'm talking about here. Flesh that needs to be loved ...

Toni Morrison, *Beloved*[1]

Despite the fact that we have woken up in them every day of our lives, our bodies, the very flesh we wear, our 'birthday suits' are perhaps the things we pay the least attention to. Many of us do not love, adequately tend to or know our bodies as well as we could. Perhaps we would even be surprised at what parts of our bodies look like, or feel like when seen or touched by the eyes or hands of another – yet it is we who live in them, and have done so our entire lives. Our bodies are sites of memory, of transgenerational trauma and of contradiction. We pray with them, experience sickness in them, grieve with them, reach ecstasy in them and at the end of everything surrender them, or rather have them surrendered by the bodies we have known and loved, to flames or to the earth when we die. We live in this knowledge that our bodies, no matter how much we love or detest them, are both our own and not our own – that they are matter that we must one day lay down. Though we are made from dust and will return to dust, we spend our lives in our bodies mostly running away from this fact, and even doing things to deny our bodies natural ageing processes through the use of serums and surgery. The beauty of our bodies for some of us is a source of pride, and for those who see no beauty in them they can be a source of shame, humiliation, pain and hardship. Most of us only know our bodies as flesh that has been faithful to us, carrying us where we need to be, bending into the shapes we put them in, enduring our clumsiness and stupidity. Yet we have seen or witnessed those whose bodies are frail and weak – who may feel that their bodies are no longer keeping their word. Only grace can hold us together when Black begins to crack, and sickness takes hold of us. It is grace that tells us that we are more than our appearance – that our value in God is unchanging, that we are more than enough in the eyes of God whose gaze can become the only one that matters. This attention to our bodies is something that Womanist scholars in particular have been helping to push us towards. Phillis Sheppard, a Womanist practical theologian and psychotherapist, does so beautifully when she remarks:

> We need to consider 'the body' in the context of a socie-ty where certain bodies are exploited to create a desire for commodities regardless of the need or ability to afford them; where the color of our skin continues to greatly influence our quality of life, our experiences in society, and our eco-nomic locations ... where sex and sexuality are used to sell 'entertainment' infused with violence. We need to hear what the body has to tell us about being created in the image of God.[2]

As a society we have decided whose bodies matter and whose bodies do not. Whose bodies are fully 'functional' and whose bodies are less than. Whose bodies are desirable and whose bodies are undesirable. We live in a world in which the body has been abused not just in history but in the present. Crucified, drowned, burned, torn apart. This is part of the body's contra-diction, its paradox, its beauty, its grace – that it is the site of so much. As children, most of us are taught about how to keep our bodies clean, tidy and presentable more than we are taught to enjoy the freedom of walking bare foot upon a moist lawn or paddling in a brook. Bodies are things that are kept, managed and controlled. Although not a universal experience by any means, when you stop and ponder this for those of us for whom it is true, and reflect deeply on its consequences, you realize that not only does our bodily neglect make no sense, it is fundamentally something we cannot afford to do for ever without some great cost both to ourselves and the other bodies around us. Your body has held the unseen you for however many years you have lived, survived perhaps, on this earth;

your body has persisted, through things it should not have, bended itself into the shape you have shaped it into, held stresses and strains, and still through it all persisted. It deserves your attention, your love, your care.

Although we have already seen in earlier chapters that grace is, in Christ, an embodied thing, it is important to explicitly say here that the grace of God is not only in the Body of Christ but, because of where Christ placed his body, grace is embodied too in the sacred bodies of Black lesbian, gay, bisexual, trans and Queer people. The doctrine of the incarnation and the grace that flows from Christ's birth and death and resurrection really has no currency if our bodies, Black and Queer, along with all other bodies, are not connected to the doctrine of the 'imago Dei' the image of God. When in Genesis 1.31 we hear that 'God saw everything that [God] had made, and indeed, it was very good', we must hear this about our flesh and all the flesh in the bodies around us.

There has been a tendency however, in Church communities, particularly Black Church communities where White culture has had a dominating control, of viewing our Black Queer bodies as sites of sin, evil and lust. In these spaces, the Black Queer body becomes a scapegoat similar to the scapegoat of Leviticus 16.21–22, which, on the day of atonement, has hands laid upon it by those wanting to be 'holy' and 'pure' to the extent that 'all [their] iniquities ... all their transgressions, all their sins' are laid upon it until it is driven out into the wilderness. The Black Queer body in the Christian community so often takes the place of this scapegoat – heterosexual Christians, having identified the location of 'sinfulness' in bodies other than their own, rid themselves of their need of grace and forgiveness, leaving the Black Queer body apparently in need of a redemption of which the heterosexual has no need. We, as Black Queer bodies, are often the scapegoat and the sacrificial offering (Leviticus 16.27) – we are both harmed by our exclusion and then also find ourselves in an exile and wilderness that we have not chosen. It is here that we begin to see our bodies as we have been told to see them. It is here that we can develop low self-esteem, self-hatred and shame. This shame makes the wilderness a preferable place to be, because to return 'home' is to return to those who see us as 'unclean'. The profound sickness of exclusive Christian communities is that as they create environments that teach us to be ashamed of ourselves and to despise our bodies, that sense of shame is then used as evidence for the 'sin' of non-heterosexual sexuality or gender identity. To call the Church 'sex-negative' is not accurate enough a description of the kind of stance it takes towards us as Black LGBTQ+ people, because the inclusion we seek goes beyond our sex lives. We must call the Church 'body-phobic', 'pleasure-denying' and 'freedom-fearing' if we are truly to get to the heart of its negative attitudes towards the LGBTQ+ community. Whatever our theologies of sex might be, the image of the chaste Black body is a problematic one when left unchallenged. What does it mean for Black LGBTQ+ bodies to deny themselves the pleasure of intimacy, of romance, of sex in a White racist world where the 'respectability' of the Black body is already demanded in every space? What does it mean for Black LGBTQ+ bodies to engage in spiritual practices that cause low self-esteem, self-hatred, even suicide in a world where Black bodies are already endangered? How is it that although Jesus never opens his mouth once in any of the four Gospels regarding homosexuality, that the one real criterion for salvation (despite what the Church says officially) is the discipline of homoerotic desire and the upholding of gender binaries? It seems to me that if we want to be set free from the entanglements that our fear of the body has led us into, we must trust more what our bodies really tell us when they experience freedom, pleasure and love.

Because of the body-phobia so prevalent in Western Christianity, we continually neglect to realize that Jesus had a body – and not a mystical body but a real body. That his body was the place that helped him feel what it meant to be human in the world, and to navigate that world as we all do. Part of our wrestling with our bodies as sites of contradiction is that we often feel this distinctly in relation to our sexuality because we separate our bodies from our souls. In the opening of his book on embodiment and theology, Paul J. Griffiths writes:

Human flesh, like all other flesh, is neither what it could be nor what it should be. It suffers and dies; is subject to disease from within and wounds from without; and finds itself in an apparently uncaring world to which it feels itself unnecessary. It is a disappointment to itself, and the care and maintenance of that disappointment require unremitting and debilitating effort.[3]

Black Queer flesh, unlike all other flesh, is neither allowed to be what it could be nor given the space to be what it should be. As Queer people, we have it communicated to us from before we know what sexual desire is, that we must exist within the definitions in which others seek to place us. We are told, taught and forced into methods of existence and patterns of living that instruct us to ignore our bodies until we can control them, or control them so that others can ignore them. Either way, our bodies come to us packaged in the clothing of an opponent.

As Black Queer people we live with a deep awareness that our bodies already evoke a certain kind of dominating and restricting gaze of super surveillance or seduction, and there is nothing in my mind that says that the same White police officer stopping and searching you, patting down the inside of your thigh for the fourteenth time on that same busy stretch of High Road, isn't getting a kick out of it in more ways than one. From Sarah Baartman to the present day, White people have been obsessed with the Black body, and sought its domination with the sanction of the Church, along with its control and annihilation, all while heteronormative culture has been uneasy about LGBTQ+ self-expression and freedom. We become aware so early on of how other bodies react to the freedom of our own flesh, and the confidence with which many of us are willing to inhabit it.

This obsession with the Black body such that it draws the gaze of others has real effects, often devastating consequences, on how we as Black people live. It manifests itself in young Black children being made aware so early on that we come to our parents or whoever is raising us drenched in vulnerability as those who are inherently endangered. There are so many occasions that come to mind when I can recall saying, 'Nan,

I'm going to meet my friends at the park, is that OK?' only to be met with 'Park? 1995 they killed *insert name of Black kid*, I don't want that to be you. Stay inna di house and mek your friends dem com'here!' To think that this sense of being endangered in this world stops at the limits of our Blackness is to misunderstand the issue for those of us who are Black and LGBTQ+. A distinct memory of mine is coming home from a shopping trip, around the age of 15, with a T-shirt I had picked up in H&M, only for it to be hidden as soon as it was discovered that very day. The T-shirt was pink, and my nan joined forces with my mother to ensure that the T-shirt disappeared before I could go out in it. When I finally realized what was going on, I faced them and asked where it was and why it had vanished from the bag minutes after entering the house with it. Their reasoning? 'If you go out in that, you will attract weird men to you.' I was too young to know (in the flesh) what they meant, but old enough to know that they knew I knew what they meant. I'd grown up to discover that certain men got excited if you held their gaze and smiled for too long, that that look meant something that words didn't have time to express. I knew too that I was attractive to other men; I had learnt this and known it. Receiving compliments on my lips or figure, or experiencing moments when 'straight' boys jokingly gestured to wanting to do what they did with their girlfriends with you, but that joke being shrouded in hidden intent laced with curiosity. It was only recently when, reflecting on my first ever time going to Pride in London, my best friend spelt out the fact that when that older White man learnt that it was our first time at Pride and then proceeded to put his hands down my trousers it wasn't funny but actually sexual assault. Our Black LGBTQ+ bodies, even in Queer-affirming spaces, can elicit danger, abuse and risk. The Black body in the White imagination is fetishized and regularly used as that upon which White fantasies are played out. Even in pornography, the Black male body being fixed to notions of the 'thug' or 'beast' perpetuates this idea that the Black body is unfeeling, less than human, and made to be brutalized and brutalized.

Of all the Black bodies reflected in the LGBTQ+ spectrum, however, it is the Black trans body that is perhaps the most neglected, misunderstood, contested and vulnerable, both within and without the Church. It is important to remember that transgender people can of course be heterosexual, lesbian, gay, bisexual and asexual, because trans identity relates to gender rather than sexual attraction or orientation. The Black, Queer, writer, performer and theatre-maker Travis Alabanza has spoken about what trans means to them, the way in which it speaks to freedom and independence:

> When I say trans, I also mean escape. I mean choice. I mean autonomy. I mean wanting something greater than what you told me. Wanting more possibilities than the one you forced on me.

When it comes to reflecting on the Black trans body, we must appreciate that more than any other this Black body is one at risk of violence from the moment of birth until death. Trans lives are immediately vulnerable as, although easily forgotten, it is in the delivery room that babies have a sex given to them by virtue of their genitalia. The dividing up of human beings into severely defined categories begins at birth, but what about those for whom the assigned sex isn't right? The reality is that:

> Everything from science, to culture, to common wisdom affirms to us that there are only two options to choose from: male and female. These categories refer to our 'biological makeup'. To deviate from either option is [seen as] unnatural and to 'journey' from one to another is sacrilege.[4]

Here, Lola Olufemi's use of the word sacrilege is particularly interesting. For me, it evokes the power of religious language in relation to the various bodies that exist in the world. The use of the term sacrilege to describe how others see gender transition reminds us of how theological language lands upon particular people in powerful, all-encompassing ways and how from the earliest times of our existence this language can define and determine our lives. 'Sacrilege' as a word essentially means violation or misuse of what is regarded as sacred; it is similar to other words such as desecration, profanity, blasphemy and sin. All of these are theologically infused words, they relate to and evoke God and God's laws. Notions of deviance, sacrilege and the unnatural have deep theological connotations and they position the body, when used to define it, as that which is barren of the divine goodness that grace imparts on to every body, not excluding trans bodies. Not only are trans people under particular suffering at this time in our world due to physical violence, the trans body is also the locus for violent discussion and debate. While trans people are viewed as deviant and disruptive for the ways in which, through their courageous inhabiting of themselves as they truly are, they challenge the norms of gender and the societal roles that ideas of gender come with. In myriad ways trans folk face, often alone, the severity of those who hold to the 'idea that women are born and not made or named'.[5] For those who believe this, the Black trans body becomes a battle ground for those committed to gender essentialism (the idea that gender is an innate, intrinsic and fixed quality of men and women) and those who perpetuate anti-Blackness – neither of which are disconnected from toxic uninterrogated Christian theologies. When we interrogate some of these views, particularly the view that gender is a fixed, innate and intrinsic quality of women and men, we can discover thoughts rooted in illiterate understanding of the Genesis creation narratives involving Adam and Eve, theological ideas that shape and fix our reception of traditions such as marriage, Christian ministry and how life functions within Christian community where gender roles are often firmly fixed. From our understanding of what a Christian priest looks like to our separate 'Men' and 'Women's' Fellowship, to who is often found in a church kitchen at a social event or providing the refreshments on a Sunday, we can see how our ideas of gender affect our very lives within the Body of Christ. Ultimately, there is nothing held by a religious tradition, no way that a religious tradition shapes its life or inhabits space, that only affects the 'members' of that tradition, and the exclusion of trans individuals from the centre of the Church's reflections on human sexuality fails to take this relationship between Christian legacies, Christian life and trans life in the present day seriously.

Our societal ideas around whose body is 'acceptable' and

whose bodies we feel we 'understand' have very real, everyday impacts upon trans people. While we can focus on the very real fact that gender non-conforming people regularly face harassment, harm and abuse – that they die daily and are positioned for this abuse, for this deathly existence, from the moment their sex is assigned – we must remember the (what might appear as less violent) forms of prejudice and discrimination that relate to the use of toilets, changing rooms and even employment. Behind all of this, colonial legacies tied up with the violence of some Christian thought distort histories, cultural practices and societal norms within which gender may have, and is often proven to have, operated in much more fluid, transgressive and ultimately life-giving ways. In a number of previous colonial powerhouses, penal laws regarding homosexuality and other non-heteronormative existences have remained. Meanwhile, the West seeking to forget the sordid and barbaric behaviour in its not-so-distant past has the gall to claim progress in a world that leaves Black and Brown countries appearing to be playing 'catch up' with so-called 'civilized' countries. It is Black and Brown bodies that continue to bear the weight of the colonial legacy in its various past playgrounds, and Black and Brown bodies that are left to undo these harmful legacies in those places where LGBTQ+ people face oppression for who they are. While being transgender and being intersex are two very different things – the first relating to identity and the second relating to one's physical body – intersex people are also largely forgotten when discussing human sexuality and gender identity. In thinking through the ways in which bodies suffer and experience harm it is telling that statistics in the UK about intersex people were very hard to find in 2019:

> The British government has said it is unaware how many intersex children – those born with bodies that do not conform to standard notions of male or female – are being subjected to surgeries on the NHS ... These include operations for which there is no medical need and where no consent has been obtained from the patient. It can lead to young patients effectively being assigned a sex that they may not identify with.[6]

This lack of data collection exists despite both the UN Convention Against Torture and the World Health Organization publicly opposing surgery to 'normalize' infants when there is no medical basis, and in 2017 Great Ormond Street Hospital concluded that its treatment of such patients was 'failing' them and 'not meeting care standards'.[7] The understandings of what we deem as 'normal' in this society are shaped heavily by our religious traditions and inheritance; with 1.7 per cent of the population estimated to have some form of intersex variation, each human body must be afforded the basic human right and dignity that comes with being made in the image of God. Sean Saifa Wall, a Black intersex activist and public researcher, writes movingly about his own experience of being born intersex, and how at the age of 25, having received his medical records after months of waiting, he discovered:

> In the records was written: 'In the interest of proper psychosexual orientation of the infant, and in order to protect the parent's emotional wellbeing, the mother has been told that: 1. The baby is a girl and will function as such. 2. She has gonads which require removal in the future (not testes).'

Wall goes on to say:

> My mother would later tell me that when she brought me home from the hospital the Pediatric Endocrinology Clinic harassed her for a couple of weeks about bringing me in for surgery to remove my undescended testes. She wondered, 'Why are these people harassing me so much?' My mother's resistance alone spared me from surgery until I was much older.[8]

The resistance of Black mothers having to intervene against systems so committed to half-understandings of the human that can be lethal to us should not go unnoticed. Like God's love, the love of our Black elders has in so many cases been the protecting guard around us against systems of multiple oppressions. Within the LGBTQ+ spectrum, perhaps it is our trans, intersex and non-binary kin who at this time most need this protection against concepts of sex and gender that seek to disable rather than enable their existence. Indeed even within the LGB communities transphobic and queerphobic attitudes remain, which too often go unchallenged. This harmful reality is seen clearly in the existence of the LGB Alliance, a 'group of lesbians, gay men and bisexuals' whose website states:

> We believe that biological sex is observed in the womb and/ or at birth and not assigned. In our view, current gender ideologies are pseudo-scientific and present a threat to people whose sexual orientation is towards the same sex, in the case of bisexuals, to both sexes. In addition, we believe that these ideologies are confusing and dangerous to children.[9]

The LGB Alliance's connection to organizations such as the Christian Institute, for example, show how this toxic mix of transphobia and the Christian Right often come together to set upon those who are easy targets within the LGBTQ+ community. Lola Olufemi makes the link between 'TERFs' – Trans Exclusionary Radical Feminists – and the Church in coming together in establishing the strict gender codes that perpetuate harm:

> Whether through policing public bathrooms or making access to medical transition harder than it should be, they align themselves with the church and the state (who are not natural allies to feminists) in order to legitimize their agenda.[10]

In its silence, or ambiguity around LGBTQ+ life as valid and equal, the Church sends the message that God's mind is not made up on LGBTQ+ lives, and that our bodies carry the potential not to be sacred. As a trans ally and Christian leader, I see it as crucial that those in my position communicate the fact that Blackness and trans-ness are not contradictions and that both have a place within the Christian community. I must acknowledge that gender is often the site of injustice, and therefore as a cis-gendered gay man in a deeply transphobic society, it is a duty to proclaim that 'Christianity is about a message of radical, boundary-destroying love. Christianity, rightly understood, is about the transgression of boundaries. Christians believe in a God whose love undoes every binary'.[11]

What becomes evident from some Christian responses to the LGBTQ+ community is that ultimately there is a great unease around those of us who push the boundaries of gender and sexuality – that our very existence makes parts of the Christian community, and even those who consider themselves nominally Christian within society, uncomfortable. Kelly Brown Douglas asks a pertinent question and offers an elucidating answer in relation to this: 'What is the problem in the church? It is a body problem. And, to have a body problem is to have a crisis of identity.'[12] It is hard not to see this crisis of identity in relation to the Church's body-phobia as rooted in the clear sense of identity that many of us in the LGBTQ+ communities have. In part this could be because our identities are challenged so forcefully that we spend a lot of time doing the inner work of discovering not just who we truly are but who we want to become. This inner work leaves us more aware than many of the people we find ourselves surrounded by in the Church, whose identities and expressions of self are perhaps less contested. Whether we see this in conservative evangelical Christians[13] who seek to abolish sex work because it is sinful, but remain body-phobic and homophobic, and fail to comprehend how their denomination's own language around sexuality contributes to unhealthy sexual practice, or in Black-majority Churches that can be regularly capitalist and in many cases locked into White Supremacist politics, we see that 'Christian' attitudes to both the body and gender have an impact in a very particular way on how LGBTQ+ people live and experience life in a way that is unique and not at all comparable to heterosexual Christian life. It is because of this that such power exists in those of us who are Black Christian and Queer living this truth openly within and beyond the walls of a church that is destabilized by our very presence. The Black lesbian activist and scholar Angela Davis, in saying that the 'process of trying to assimilate into an existing category in many ways runs counter to efforts to produce radical or revolutionary results',[14] reminds us of how fundamental it is for us to remain Queer bodies in a religious institution that so desperately needs to become Queer itself – in becoming Queer, the Church that is the Body of Christ truly inhabits Christ's own character but becomes the kind of body that can allow others in. The Black Catholic theologian M. Shawn Copeland remarks: 'The only body capable of taking us *all* in as we are with all our different body marks – certainly including the mark of homosexuality – is the body of Christ.'[15] These marks in my own mind include the very scars of those trans beloved who have had the required surgery to make them whole, waiting on lists or raising funds to enable them to live in the freedom so many of us who are cisgendered take for granted. In Christ's body we are, each of us, called to enter without erasure, censure or subjugation – it is Christ the wounded and risen healer who welcomes us with our wounds, scars and histories. To belong to the Body of Christ is to bring our bodies into the place and person who welcomes us without the erasing of our differences, the one who sees us in all our diversity and loves us anyway – one who calls us to see ourselves and Christ in the beauty of the other.

However much we might believe the Church to be a place in which all bodies can find themselves at home, we know that this is not yet the case in so many contexts. Particularly problematic is the way in which our theologies both sung and spoken impact our understandings of the body, but also enable us to think that we are achieving that which is actually an aspiration within the Church. A particularly popular Christian hymn that makes this point perfectly and is frequently sung with fervour and zeal is the song 'Let us build a house where love can dwell', the fourth verse of which reads:

> Let us build a house where hands will reach beyond the
>   wood and stone
> to heal and strengthen, serve and teach, and live the Word
>   they've known.
> Here the outcast and the stranger bear the image of
>   God's face;
> Let us bring an end to fear and danger.
> All are welcome, all are welcome,
>   All are welcome in this place.[16]

As beautiful as this hymn (and others like it) might be, I think it important to remember that for those of us who are Black, Queer and Christian they speak more to an eschatological (end time) hope than a present reality. They are evocative of the vision we are offered in Revelation 7.9 where a great uncountable multitude from every nation, tribe, people and language stand before God. Not enough Christian communities ask themselves when singing hymns like this the important questions: what bodies are being welcomed into this space? Which bodies are considered the 'outcast' or the 'stranger'? What might we, the existent gathered community, need to sacrifice for all bodies to be welcome? Which bodies do we truly believe bear the image of God, and what are the terms and conditions we communicate as necessary for accessing God's grace? Often, I am left in the midst of existing church communities reflecting on the corporeal absence of many LGBTQ+ friends whose Black Queer bodies are not only regularly absent, but would be made anything but welcome. Rowan Williams writes in his essay 'The Body's Grace':

> Grace, for the Christian believer, is a transformation that depends in large part on knowing yourself to be seen in a certain way: as significant, as wanted. The whole story of creation, incarnation, and our incorporation into the fellowship of Christ's body tells us that God desires us, as if we were God, as if we were that unconditional response to God's giving that God's self makes in the life of the Trinity. We are created so that we may be caught up in this; so that we may grow into the wholehearted love of God by learning that God loves us as God loves God. The life of the Christian community has as its rationale – if not invariably its practical reality – the teaching us so to order our relations that human beings may see themselves as desired, as the occasions of joy.[17]

Williams' definition of grace has at its heart three focal points. Grace, for the Christian believer, is about transformation, self-knowledge and desire. The Christian, says Williams, is transformed not solely by an encounter with the divine, transcendent reality of God, but through a shift in self-knowledge, through a shift in outlook upon one's self which takes place within Christian community. The transformation from one state of being, which may have been to see oneself as insignificant, despised and rejected, to seeing oneself as 'significant, as wanted'. And Williams goes further, to say that that shift in outlook upon oneself, that new self-knowledge, that re-perception comes about by hearing, feeling, seeing what the whole story of creation and incarnation has to say to us, about us. That story is told to us through our incorporation into the fellowship of Christ's body, which ought to tell us that we are above all desired, loved and created to be caught up in that mystery that is God Trinity. Despite Williams' understanding of grace to be about transformation, it is it seems primarily about the transformation of the individual believer. And, for the Black LGBTQ+ Christian, the invitation to transformation often presents itself as the requirement to leave your Queer body, with all of its desire, at the door. One of the first potential barriers to the reception of Black Queer bodies in the ecclesial community (the Church) might be the way in which we approach grace.

If grace is primarily something by which I – the Black Queer Christian – am changed, is my transformation a prerequisite, or a response, to basking in the grace of God? And if grace is prevenient, which I would insist it is, how are our Queer Black bodies to navigate grace if it is so frequently packaged in exclusive and elusive clothing? Whenever a Black LGBTQ+ Christian encounters spaces that have a particular understanding of purity as the defining note of holiness, a high view of the ministry that presents the person at the front as the sole interpreter of scripture, where baptism is seen as the death of sin rather than to sin, and respect for one's elders leads to any sexual discourse being curtailed, grace will seldom be understood as being for all. It can be very difficult to bring the whole of ourselves before a God who apparently, in Jesus Christ, died for the whole of you and your being when you are encouraged to leave significant portions of you outside a specific space. Our churches can only be considered holy spaces when we are able to bring our whole selves into them. It is the mark of a mature church that it is able to embrace all people regardless of the stories they embody, the truths they seek to share and the love they yearn to express. We could say that the key to keeping Christian communities alive as centres of mature love and authentic worship is their capability to grow into authentically honest communities, where together the diverse people of God live and encourage one another to keep on 'telling the truth – the truth about what we see, what we feel, what we really want ... Mature love requires us to acknowledge our full experience, our feelings and wants, while making grown-up choices about them.'[18]

In any ecclesial community – particularly in the Black-majority but White-led churches in the UK where the leadership of a church may be entirely male, heterosexual and tied up with patriarchal ways of reading scripture – the unspoken barriers to God's grace for LGBTQ+ bodies can be numerous. These spaces are contexts in which there is often grace for men and condemnation for women when it comes to sexual 'misconduct', spaces in which it is often accepted that the worshipping community is a place in which men (married or single, but always 'straight') can come to seek a future intimate partner or spouse so long as 'Bible-distance' is maintained. These are spaces in which newborns of heterosexual couples are celebrated with great pomp as 'good bodies', where single men and single women receive spiritual nurture in separate spaces because it is assumed they cannot quite keep their hands and eyes off each other, and where male effeminacy or female masculinity are treated as highly suspicious, unless of course you can sing or play keys, in which case there will always be a place for you in the choir – and there, positioned in terms of your giftedness, your fertility, infertility and sexuality are no longer any of our business. In many Black churches, homosexuality can be perceived as a distinct threat not just to orthodox Christianity, but more to the Black heterosexual body, and particularly the Black family. The White politician, however, whose actual policy may pose a real and serious threat to Black lives, might find more grace and acceptance in a Black church depending on the size of their wallet – this is a particularly accurate description of Black churches in the USA.

On another level, anyone who openly owns their LGBTQ+

identity in a Black church is likely to have their Queer body and its sexuality viewed through the lens of demonology, mental disarray, or simply an appetite for sin. The poor theologies of holiness in the Christian community as being less about our attitude towards God, the transformation of our sight and the education of our desire, but more about what we do and do not do with our bodies, lead to this problem. We have churches therefore that care more, it seems, about who people may or may not fuck than they do about the food or lack of food in people's cupboards. It is implied that holiness is impossible without bodily purity – but this purity is often communicated as existing beyond the LGBTQ+ body, and beyond same-sex love. Because of this, 'Transsexual people who transition from one side of the gender binary to the other are often accepted in Church communities, so long as they are heterosexual or celibate in their new gender.'[19] Martin Luther King Jr, when warning about the new conservatism of the Black church, and all Christian churches, courageously declared: 'Nowhere is the tragic tendency to conform more evident than in the church, an institution that has often served to crystallize, conserve, and even bless the patterns of majority opinion.'[20] So grace, meted out as it is to our bodies within the Body of Christ, is often dependent on what we have or have not done with our bodies, or what we may have imagined doing. None of this is necessarily, I hasten to add, explicitly proclaimed within these spaces; rather it is promulgated by the way acceptable things – behaviour, clothing, families, love, relationships, interactions – are treated as acceptable, as 'normal'. Barbara Glasson talks about the way in which how we worship, the language we use in worship, impacts upon real life:

> If liturgy is the spoken language of the Church, then there is also the need to consider its body language. By this, I mean the way in which church communities present themselves in unspoken ways. It is said that 96 per cent of all communication is non-verbal, and this is true of institutions as well as individuals. It is these unspoken messages that often say more about mission than the words that come out of our mouth.[21]

The Church, then, must consider what its posture as a body communicates to the world. How does its shape, its language, its silence, its image communicate what is the heart of its belief to the world? Professor Ashon Crawley, an assistant professor of religious studies and African-American studies at the University of Virginia, reflects on his experience of the body language of the Church in these words:

> In that boy-child, there was something about the desire to practise comfort and care that was also an openness to worlds, an enchantment with possibility, a desire for connection to all that was and was not tangible. That desire would go on to find expression years later in my own queer sexuality, a mode of being that, like my grandmother's, the doctrines of Blackpentecostalism would certainly condemn …
>
> Growing up as a member of Blackpentecostal churches, these feelings within me took on new life. The kindness of the saints taught me about care and concern as a method for engaging others; the church showed me, in a world replete with antiblack racism, that some things are most deeply felt when one retreats into the sound of handclaps, foot stomps, tambourine and praise-noise.
>
> But the dogmas of Blackpentecostalism could also sever and forestall care. As my desire expanded into queer sexuality, I'd reflect on the doctrine that lives like mine were abominable, and the gap that produced within. I wondered about the space between the care my grandmother practised – a care I can remember only as the *feel* I have for her – and the eternal torment I understood to be her denouement.
>
> Blackpentecostalism is a site of such gaps and contradictions, at least as I theorise it.[22]

For Crawley, the Church and its language – both spoken and unspoken – were simultaneously a place of retreat and a place lacking in care. As his desire expressed itself in queer sexuality he had to begin to reflect on what he calls the 'doctrine' that rendered his life and lives like his 'abominable'. We too know the gap that rendering of our lives and desire produces within us, the space we feel it places between us and God. We too know the eternal torment that comes when the Church tells us our bodies and identity are sinful. In the same spaces where the grace of God is proclaimed, taught and assumed, there is a contradiction, a dualism. Grace as currently expressed in the Christian community often lacks in generosity towards the LGBTQ+ body rendering itself ineffective. Many who feel a desire to participate in the fullness of Black Christian community, to 'practise comfort and care', to feed that 'desire for connection' which Ashon Crawley speaks of, often find that walls have been drawn around them through a process of trickle-down 'grace-onomics' – that they are now on the outside of the Church looking in, having discovered that 'all' are in fact not welcome in this place. In her work on sexuality and the Black Church, Kelly Brown Douglas connects some of what Ashon Crawley expresses:

> The same way in which White cultural narratives caricature Black people, the sanctified narrative of the Black church caricatures LGBTQ people. They are people considered driven by the lustful passions of their bodies. They are seen as lewdly out of control. Hence, these are bodies that have been shunned and ignored by the Black church. The result is not only the inner conflict and turmoil it creates for LGBTQ peoples, but also the way it literally kills these Black bodies.[23]

The Church both Black and White becomes a place that in essence is more accepting of violence and exclusion than it is same-sex love.

How then does grace change things? Can the grace of God be wide enough to encompass, embrace, encourage and enrich the lives of Black Queer people and the bodies we bring? While the historically dominant tradition of the Church tends to demonize the flesh, and the Church's collusion with White Supremacy resulted in the demonizing of Black flesh in particular, the doctrine of the incarnation has made some things clear about our bodies, and therefore our lives. First, that our flesh matters and, second, that that flesh has been redeemed in a Black and wounded Christ. In seeing the violence of the cross so clearly displayed on Jesus, we see the truth about the

condition of our lives both within and beyond the Church –
Jesus too was wounded by those who professed to believe in
God and who, like the people of God today, failed to practise
love. The image of Christ on the cross speaks profoundly to
what we in our Black LGBTQ+ bodies know and have experienced. The gaping wounds of Christ have something to say to
the gaping wounds of those Black bodies that have found themselves wounded (often physically) by a misuse of the gospel,
and the silence of the Church. The arms outstretched display
for all to see the incarnation of the God who reaches out to all
the corners of the earth with grace, of which there is enough
for thousands, because if there is not it is not grace. Grace is
that through which our collective lives and institutional lives
may be transformed. Our understandings of holiness so often
being tied up with individual purity need to be transformed to
thinking about our institutional sanctification rather than the
transformation of individual bodies. To accept that we are 'born
this way' is to wrestle with the reality that God cannot redeem
that which is *not* you because that person does not exist, and
if individuals are being encouraged to be transformed to the
point that they are no longer themselves, then grace becomes
unworkable because God cannot bless who we pretend to be.
Our institutions, then, need to practise the repentance they so
often call for in the lives of LGBTQ+ individuals. The lack of
existing safe worship spaces for Black LGBTQ+ Christians in
the UK tells something of the fact that Black Queer bodies do
not feel free in the Church. Even those pressure groups that
are working towards full LGBTQ+ inclusion in the Church
are often operating under an all-White leadership. The challenge in terms of transformation for these bodies may be a
transformation not only of the institution's heart but also of
its imagination. Even a church that re-perceives itself as it truly
is, as having profoundly and vigorously participated in the
oppression of others, may find in its repentance the awesome
grace of God. In the final chapter, I explore some of what the
future will be like if the Church fails to engage with this work
of repentance and reparation.

For the Black Queer Christian, beyond all that the Church
has said to contradict the dignity of the human person, the

most profound contradiction of the dignity of the Black body is the transatlantic slave trade. Only those failing to follow the trajectory of time could fail to see that White Supremacy could never have flourished so profoundly if Whiteness had never become synonymous with 'God'. Over the years, the White body has been seen to be emblematic of holiness, over and above that of the Black body. We absorb White Supremacy in theological language and metaphors, even in holy scripture. To a certain degree, White Supremacy is Christianity's child that it has never acknowledged as its own blood. Yet day by day, the features of this child are coming to bear upon White Supremacy's adult face and the resemblance is unavoidable. In the Church, White Supremacy has been canonized in a racist society and a racist Church – one that has made Jesus, and by extension God, White. To pretend as though this does not impact upon the White mind in a world where Black life is fragile is a delusion. How the Church has depicted its Lord for centuries has transfigured the White gaze when it lands upon us – and to many we are considered inferior. To begin to connote Blackness with the beautiful is to begin to exorcise the violent and all-pervasive supremacy of Whiteness from its multifarious lodgings. In a world adjusted to the suffering Black body, it should be considered not just holy but necessary work. It should be no surprise that in the hands of Whiteness, a theology of grace extending to the Black body becomes, in the hands of too many White theologians, a convenient means to peace, or silence – so malleable that Black folk are asked to show grace, the very grace we have yet to witness in White people's treatment of us both past and present. In Whiteness we see perfectly what it looks like when grace is taken for granted, and when God becomes locked into a transactional, functionally capitalist system in which the Black LGBTQ+ non-conformist is always in theological debt and spiritual defi-cit. In 2020, the murder of George Floyd led to many White Christians finally finding their voice against racism, yet there is still a great contradiction and hypocrisy in a church that has learnt to say aloud that 'Black Lives Matter'; fundamentally the contradiction exists in the fact that it does not truly believe that, because it is part of the violent forces that stop Black people breathing. The depth of anti-Black violence, and the Church's complicit role in anti-Black and anti-LGBTQ+ violence, shows that this tragic fact is not truly realized.

The African American writer Ta-Nehisi Coates puts it this way:

All our phrasing [of] race relations, racial chasm, racial justice, racial profiling, white privilege, even white supremacy – serves to obscure that racism is visceral experience, that it dislodges brains, blocks airways, rips muscle, extracts organs, cracks bones, breaks teeth. You must never look away from this. You must always remember that the sociology, the history, the economics, the graphs, the charts, the regressions all land, with great violence, upon the body.[24]

The Church's problem here is one of controlled engagement in which it will only face the bodies it harms when it has the upper hand and is in control. The issue with establishing more commissions and committees[25] or their equivalent in an effort to deal with racial injustice, as it has done, is that it buys into the lie that the time for discourse is not yet over. Personally, I think it is a myth to believe that there is anything more to say when it comes to race and the Christian Church. The demand on the White Church is quite simple: we are asking you to be more like Jesus, to let us breathe, to let us sit as equal kin at the table. It's only difficult because, if you're honest, you do not want to give up your power and privilege. The real question is: can any of us be truly redeemed, truly sanctified while holding on to a power that is not ours and that directly impacts vulnerable bodies? Or, is there a kenotic demand at the heart of the gospel? A demand made by the body of Jesus – that it will not do for some to carry crosses while others carry feathers. That the White Christian too must use their body, 'take up their cross and follow' Jesus, and quit faking discipleship.

That so many factions of the Church fail to notice the absence of openly Black LGBTQ+ Christians in their midst is sad enough, but what is tragic, indeed sinful, is that so many Black Queer Christians live in a bodily exile that they have been forced into. This exile is twofold – an exile from the body of Christ and an exile from what the LGBTQ+ community portrays as its mainstream. The LGBTQ+ movement however, unlike the church, is not under a mandate to love all people. The Body of Christ has become the place where

> We force our children out of the wholeness and connected-ness in which they begin their lives. Instead of cultivating intimacy ... we teach boys and girls, in complementary ways, to bury their deepest selves, to stop speaking, or attending to, the truth, to hold in mistrust, or even in disdain, the state of closeness we all, by our natures, most crave. We live in an antirelational, vulnerability-despising culture, one that not only fails to nurture the skills of connection but actively fears them.[26]

Rather than being bound together in love, our bodies within the Christian community are often separated. For Black Christians this bodily separation is ancient – one could even say that the Church as it is today was never built with us as free people in mind. Since the time of slavery, British Christian history has been one of 'God fearing men going about their godless business', to quote historian James Walvin.[27] This locationality means that our bodies by their very existence within the Body of Christ will always point out, through being Black and Queer, all the fallacies of institutional Christianity. That our bodies are not so much sites of the truth but places in which the truth of the gospel is revealed to the extent that it is lived out wherever we are made welcome. Black Queer bodies can never be safe within any institution that is anti-freedom, anti-inclusion, anti-love because our bodies demand all these things in order to thrive.

What we do with our bodies has both political and deeply theological consequences. We are used to hearing of these consequences as being inherently negative, but I wonder if there is – in our Queer embodiment – a way of being that points to the liberation that comes from knowing Christ? JJ Bola is a writer who in the UK pushes our ideas of what Black masculinity looks like, often encouraging men to speak from a place of emotional vulnerability, to explore intimacy and embrace. In his book *Mask Off: Masculinity Redefined*, he writes about the way in which the Christian faith impacts the way we understand gender:

> I was raised in a religious background: Congolese/African culture is very religious, with Christianity dominating in the sub-Saharan region in particular. The notion of gender or sexual fluidity was taught to me as abhorrent or deviant from the way that the world was created or meant to be, long before I even developed a sexual orientation of my own; imagine being a five year old boy who is told that any boy who likes another boy will burn in hell forever – it is a terrifying thought. When I eventually removed myself from what I was taught and began to read into spiritual and religious belief that existed before Christianity, or other Abrahamic faiths, and pre-colonial societies, I learned of just how normal and accepted gender and sexual fluid people were in more ancient societies.[28]

Those of us who push the boundaries of this inherited White Christian concept of what is right and wrong for the Black body participate in a radical work of undoing. It is transgressive for us to relocate our bodies, with their same-sex desire, as sites of the sacred and the Christian. To say this is to say that until we explicitly associate Queerness with holiness and Blackness with the sacred our Black LGBTQ+ bodies cannot be safe in the Church. Essentially, until then, we exist simply as those whose bodies are beyond what those with power and privilege see as having divine dignity, value and worth. To be transgressive not only in terms of the sex we choose to have, but also the gender identities that we inhabit, might be to place us closer to the Jesus who was viewed as both radical and deviant. Where we place our bodies, who we share them with, how we dress them, have the capacity to be both political and theological. In the words of Pat Califia:

> being a sex radical means being defiant as well as deviant. It means being aware that there's something unsatisfying and dishonest about the way sex is talked about (or hidden)

in daily life. It also means questioning the way our society assigns privilege based on adherence to its moral codes, and in fact makes every sexual choice a matter of morality.[29]

In a very real way, Christianity is sex education. It teaches us what is 'acceptable' and 'unacceptable', 'right' and 'wrong' in relation to our bodies – often with no actual reference to the realities or nuances of life. We are taught from our first experience of God, or 'God's Word', many moral codes which both condemn and restrict us, and deny us the life-giving beauty of intimacy.

Because African Americans exist at the hegemonic centre of Blackness, Black British LGBTQ+ characters are not as well known as their African American counterparts. Writing on the invisibility of Black British LGBTQ+ people during Black History Month the writer and journalist Jason Okundaye highlights the fact that the centring of Black Britishness doesn't extend to our Queer British ancestors and that the spotlight tends to focus on those Black Queer figures such as Bayard Rustin, James Baldwin, Stormé DeLarverie and Marsha P. Johnson. He notes that prevalent among White Queer people is the idea that

> the often repeated but false statement 'Don't forget, Marsha P Johnson *threw the first brick* at Stonewall' is a method for superficially engaging with Black queerness. The focus on singular and mythical brick-throwing moments allows Black queer figures to be presented as sacrificial lambs fighting in service of a broader queer movement, rather than people operating with the primary goals of self-organisation and self-preservation. Of course, the organising of Black queer and trans people such as Marsha should be honoured and taught, but it doesn't hold much relevance to Black British queer history.[30]

When we look back through the history of Black people in the UK, it can be easy to assume that there are no people who, like us, have been both Black and LGBTQ+. The contrary of course is the reality, but as the Black Queer, androgynous doctor and TV presenter Dr Ronx Ikharia says, 'You cannot be what you cannot see.' We are everywhere but so often remain in the archives of history as those little known and frequently unlooked for. Although we might not personally be able to name many of those who in their Black LGBTQ+ identity came before us, we certainly owe any security or freedom we enjoy here to those who led the way, taking fear by the throat and walking in their truth. It's important for us to remember that it was just over 20 years ago that Justin Fashanu, a Black, gay, professional footballer born in Hackney to Nigerian and Guyanese parents took his own life. Surrounding Fashanu's premature and tragic death were multiple things but primarily a lethal cocktail of homophobia, guilt and shame. About a month or so before his suicide, Fashanu had been accused of sexually assaulting a 17-year-old in the US state of Maryland, a state in which homosexual acts were still illegal. Although he was questioned by police he was not held in custody, and by the time the police attempted their arrest he had fled to England. On 3 May 1998, aged only 37, Justin Fashanu was found hanging in a deserted garage in Shoreditch, London. In his suicide note,[31] having denied the charges against him, and stating that he fled to England because he knew he wouldn't have a fair trial in the United States he wrote:

> Being gay and a personality is so hard, but everybody has it hard at the moment, so I can't complain about that. I want to say I didn't sexually assault the young boy. He willingly had sex with me and then the next day asked for money. When I said no, he said 'you wait and see.'
>
> If that is the case, I hear you say, why did I run? Well, justice isn't always fair ... I felt I wouldn't get a fair trial because of my homosexuality ... I realised that I had already been presumed guilty. I do not want to give any more embarrassment to my friends and family.[32]

When I read the words with which Fashanu articulates the causes of his despair, I am moved deeply. In part because it is a despair that I have known and have heard many others express. Those of us who, looking out on the horizon and failing to see any hope of dawn, have surveyed the purpose of life and found little meaning. It's hard to imagine the burden Fashanu carried, having made it to the thirty-seventh year of his life as the very first professional footballer to come out as gay, but it was a burden that became in light of this allegation too much to bear. What so few people ever speak about is how Fashanu's coming out and his relationship to the Church also shaped his story and the end of that story. In an interview from the year of his death, the friend of Fashanu and human rights activist Peter Tatchell 'attributed Fashanu's decline to the hostility his homosexuality sparked and to his conversion to evangelical Christianity. Tatchell and Fashanu met at a gay club in London in 1982 and remained close friends until 1993.' Tatchell noted that Fashanu

> became very confused and unhappy about his sexuality. His attempts at relationships with women failed, and he ended up being forced into furtive, gay sexual encounters, which precluded the possibility of a stable relationship ... His religious friends insisted on him being celibate, while he still had strong desires for relationships with men. In that kind of situation, anybody could have cracked.[33]

In an interview I found from 1984, prior to his coming out, Fashanu can be seen making a case against people working on Sundays. His argument was that the Lord's commandment to 'keep the Sabbath holy' should be honoured and he particularly felt that no one should work on a Sunday to further their own cause. In the interview, when pressed as to his reasons why he has only played football on a Sunday twice, Fashanu states clearly: 'I believe that my first calling is to Jesus.'[34] Now, it might be tempting to adopt the approach of Peter Tatchell, and to see as so many might that Christianity to Justin was nothing but a stifling rock upon him. That the Christian faith as he had inherited it was not a blessing but a burden. Those of us who are Black and LGBTQ+ know how often that can be the case, but I want to allow Justin's words here – words not about the Church but about Jesus – to speak. Actually, Justin in that interview serves as a public apologist bearing witness to the prophetic message of Jesus. Essentially, Justin's position was that he personally would not play on a Sunday because, beyond his pocket, that labour served no one. He mentioned a doctor working on a Sunday being acceptable because, as well as financially benefiting, her patients benefit too. What we might not remember about Justin is that he often visited churches to speak to the generation below him, and that the Church for him was never, in his own words, a burden. Often when looking into the life of another it can be all too easy to try and make their narrative neat, and therefore, in a situation like this, to assume that Fashanu's decline was due, as Tatchell says, 'to the hostility his homosexuality sparked and to his conversion to evangelical Christianity'. But beyond Fashanu's Christian friends – pushing celibacy upon him in order to make their own consciences comfortable – I am always reluctant to assess someone's relationship with God. Fashanu seems to have believed that Jesus not only spoke in the past but spoke in the here and now, and that Jesus, as he knew him, cared about our life here. Of more direct impact to Fashanu was the reaction of both his family and the Black community in relation to his coming out. In an article recounting the response of *The Voice*, the UK's only national Afro-Caribbean weekly newspaper, we hear:

> The reaction of the wider black community was just as bad. His coming out was condemned by *The Voice* as 'an affront to the black community ... damaging ... pathetic and unforgivable'.
>
> 'We heteros', wrote *Voice* columnist Tony Sewell, 'are sick and tired of tortured queens playing hide-and-seek around their closets. Homosexuals are the greatest queer-bashers around. No other group of people are so preoccupied with making their own sexuality look dirty.'[35]

It is well known that particularly painful for Fashanu was the rejection he experienced from his own community. In conversation, Peter Tatchell shared that Fashanu expressed sadness about this and told him:

that since black people knew the pain of racial prejudice and discrimination, he expected they'd be understanding and supportive. Some were, but many denounced him for bringing 'shame' on them. As far as I recall, not a single Black public figure supported his coming out or condemned *The Voice* and others in the community who had trashed him. Justin later told *The Voice*: 'Those who say that you can't be Black, gay and proud of it are ignorant.'[36]

We don't really know why Justin chose to come out when he did, some say he was about to be outed, others say he knew someone who had been forced out of their parents family home and who committed suicide, and so rather than remain quietly in the closet, Fashanu wanted to set an example to others and come out publicly in the papers. Described by his manager at Nottingham Forest, Brian Clough, as 'a bloody poof!', Justin was surrounded by both homophobia and racism in a sport that was accommodating of neither his race nor his sexuality, and that deeply regretted his Christian commitments. Caught up in a lifetime's worth of rejection, somewhere between God and gayness, a young, Black, gay man with a history of Christianity, it is no surprise that Fashanu struggled to keep on keeping on.

One of the ways I've connected with the history of Black Queer Britain is through those older friends and mentors who themselves act as living archives of this history. Whether they be older White clergy (some of whom have since left the Church or retired) with stories of Black and Brown partners who were growing up, attending or serving the church in London in the decades before my birth, or just those who were around when the AIDS crises was at its worst – the history I have received from them has come less from books and more from living people. Theirs was a world in which same-sex sexual activity was illegal, same-sex marriage and adoption did not exist, and the Gender Recognition Act was not in place. Theirs was a world that existed long before the repeal of Section 28 and a church in which the Archbishop of Canterbury, Geoffrey Fisher, spoke in support of the 1957 Wolfenden Report, saying that there existed 'a sacred realm of privacy ... into which the law, generally speaking, must not intrude ... a principle of the utmost importance for the preservation of human freedom, self-respect, and responsibility'. It was, in many ways, a different world. In terms of Black Queer Britain it is thanks to older friends like Ajamu X, the fine art photographer, archive curator and radical sex activist, that I've been rooted in this history and felt a personal connection to it. Ajamu, who has dedicated his life to documenting Black Queer British experience from the 1980s onwards, is the person from whom I learn where it is that Black Queer people have existed, in London particularly – where they have found, nurtured and lost (through gentrification) intimacy and love. Ajamu is the one who personally for me has challenged most the idea that Jamaican culture is inherently homophobic. He has opened my eyes to the realities of Black Queer Caribbean life, in Britain in particular, with all its complexity and nuance. Whether it is stories of Black men eliciting the interest of other Black men at Jamaican funerals, hearing about the cruising ground called 'The Church' in Brixton, or pushing the easy assumptions I have made about Black Queer British relationships with Christian spirituality, it is through his art that I see our culture(s) anew.

In a certain sense when I think about Black Queer British History I don't necessarily think of those who were born in the UK, but more those who have been Black, Queer and resident in Britain for a long or short time. Earliest in my mind is Claude McKay (1889–1948). Born in 1889 in Sunny Ville, Clarendon, Jamaica, McKay was a key figure in the Harlem Renaissance, which was a major literary movement during the 1920s. As a writer he had an influence on major individuals such as James Baldwin and Richard Wright. From 1919 to 1921 McKay was based in London and in his lifetime visited Russia, Morocco and Paris. Although sexuality is never explicitly addressed in his writing, it is widely assumed that he was bisexual, and he pursued relationships with both men and women his entire life. The fact that McKay published in 1917 under the pseudonym 'Eli Edwards' bears witness to someone wrestling with both his identity and society censure. Surprisingly, towards the end of his life, McKay converts to Roman Catholicism and dies of heart failure in Chicago having worked as a teacher for a

Catholic organization. The historian Dr Gemma Romain is doing great work in helping some of these early Black Queer characters to come to the surface. In an article written with Caroline Bressey, she says:

> To understand queer identities such as McKay's, we must not solely seek to look for 'evidence' of queerness in relation to McKay's sexual relationships; queer black histories cannot just be examined by declared mentions and moments of same-sex sexuality. How McKay's queer identity surfaced and was performed is more complex. McKay's writing, which commented upon his identity or the 'queer' way in which he viewed the world and lived his life, was often implicit and subtle.[37]

A significant factor in McKay's experience of London was his introduction to England via the lens provided to him as he read English literature as a student in Jamaica. Like so many Black writers, although he did not want race to be the focus of his work, McKay's experience of racism in America and the UK shaped how he articulated his reality in Britain, in particular the colour bar that meant he could not find accommodation near to the British Museum whose reading room would have been vital to his work. His work is described as radical in its exploration of Black love, and Queer transgressive love, particularly from a poet of African heritage. His friends in London appear to have been mostly men, as he makes no mention of women, and in particular were sailors, boxers, a West Indian doctor, a Black Oxford student and a young Black Anglican priest. It is hard to know whether these men were part of a network of Black Queer individuals in Britain providing support and a sense of community to those who were otherwise out on a limb, but they are signs of a potential early Black Queer community that consisted of all kinds of individuals and where faith, sexuality and race all intersect under Queer friendship. In her book, *Race, Sexuality and Identity in Britain and Jamaica*, Dr Gemma Romain talks of Soho as a space of gay sociability and a space that allowed for cross-racial encounters. She notes that 'Soho and the East End were key areas of black settlement and socializing, including queer black socializing'.[38] Both Soho and Roman Catholicism relate too to the legacy of Patrick Nelson (1916–63). Patrick was a migrant to interwar Britain and was a Black Queer man in 1930s London. Through his correspondence with the Bloomsbury artist Duncan Grant, his one-time partner and lifelong friend, we are given a fascinating insight into Black British LGBTQ+ history, not just in London but in relation to the Caribbean, colonialism and Empire.

Following these earlier individuals, other notable people are Ivor Gustavus Cummings OBE (1931–92), and Pearl Alcock (1934–2006), who ran a cafe and an illegal shebeen 'shoobz' on 103 Railton Road, both of which were popular with the local gay community and which became a significant place for the LGBTQ+ scene, and Caribbean gay men in particular. Bernadine Evaristo mentions this in her book *Girl, Woman, Other* where she writes of the women-only bars and of 'Pearl's shebeen in Brixton on a Friday night run by Pearl, a middle-aged Jamaican woman who stripped her basement of furniture, set up a sound system and charged at the door'.[39] Recalling the kind of clients that would attend the cafe and shebeen, a White British man named Simon recalled that the venue was

> Always heaving ... a space this sort of size packed with people dancing, and there would be a bar at the end selling Heineken or cocktail type stuff, martinis and so on ... there were only one or two women there, about 80 % black men, 20 % white I suppose. Of the black guys that would go to Pearl's ... maybe half of them would be in a relationship with a white person, and half would be in a relationship with a black person.[40]

Pearl, a Black bisexual woman, eventually became an artist and her work was an avenue for her self-expression. Art has often been a form of resistance for Black Queer people, not only in writing and painting but also in photography, dance and acting. Of a different ilk, the Nigerian-born photographer Rotimi Fani-Kayode (1955–89) is someone whose work I have always loved, and who carried out his work during the peak of the AIDS crisis, speaking powerfully and prophetically to the homophobia potent in both the UK and Nigeria. Fani-Kayode, considered one of the first Black Africans to portray openly gay identity in his work, moved to London at the age of 11 to escape the Biafran war in Nigeria. In his art he boldly explores the various tensions between the different parts of his identity in his images, about which he said:

> On three counts I am an outsider: in terms of sexuality; in terms of geographical and cultural dislocation; and in the sense of not having become the sort of respectably married professional my parents might have hoped for.[41]

In photographs of himself and his partner, Alex Hirst, there is a beautiful intimacy displayed documenting Black male desire and love. Having arrived in Britain as a boy, and having eventually come out as gay, Fani-Kayode left the UK and went to New York to study fine art and photography at the Pratt Institute. It was upon his return in the mid-1980s that he started exhibiting some of his most complex and challenging work. I am captivated by the place of spirituality in Fani-Kayode's creative exploration, particularly how, as a Black gay man, he challenges people's perceptions of what is acceptably 'African'. When speaking on his rage and desire and how that relates to his work he noted that both aesthetically and ethically:

> I seek to translate my rage and my desire into new images which will undermine conventional perceptions and which may reveal hidden worlds. Many of the images are seen as sexually explicit – or more precisely, homosexually explicit. I make my pictures homosexual on purpose. Black men from the Third World have not previously revealed either to their own peoples or to the West a certain shocking fact: they can desire each other.[42]

The idea expressed here by Fani-Kayode strongly suggests that, to many, Black same-sex desire is unknown, in the sense that it is not public. In this way, Black same-sex desire essentially exists as something that lives hidden, to be revealed, and that, I think, is deeply emotive. It shows the aspect of the freedom that comes with what we do with our bodies, and the extent to which we make our bodily desires known. In a society where so much is demanded of the Black body, the choice of rendering one's sexual desire and private loves to the realm of public knowledge is sometimes the only piece of control there is, the only area of one's life where one can sometimes make a choice. Our Black Queer love is a shocking fact to those who do not consider that we too are fully human, that we, like all other people, are many things. Fani-Kayode deals not only with the human alone however. The spiritual dynamic in his work is deeply tangible and his family, of Yoruba origin, were the keepers of the shrine and priests of Ife. His early life being one shaped by oracles and communication with the Orisha rendered the spiritual no stranger within his creative output and world view. In particular, spiritual ecstasy can be seen in his work, especially in his *Bronze Head* (1987), in which a naked Black man is sitting on a Bronze Head, literally clasping the crown of the head with his ass cheeks. The positioning of the bronze head on a wooden stool places it as an object that appears to be intended for veneration, but instead it exists and is captured in this image as that which is intimately connected to the most surprising human orifice, almost as if it is being born. Fani-Kayode embraces yet subverts the spiritual image in a number of powerful ways, which allows us to open our minds to our intimate relationship with the divine, particularly in relation to our Black Queer bodies and the body of God. Speaking of his own work, Fani-Kayode says:

My identity has been constructed from my own sense of otherness, whether cultural, racial or sexual. The three aspects are not separate within me. Photography is the tool by which I feel most confident in expressing myself. It is photography therefore – Black, African, homosexual photography – which I must use not just as an instrument, but as a weapon if I am to resist attacks on my integrity and, indeed, my existence on my own terms.[43]

The instrument of his survival, his art, held Fani-Kayode well in his life in a world where the various aspects of his identity were under scrutiny both within and without the Black African community. Fani-Kayode died, aged just 34, in a London hospital of a heart attack recovering from an AIDS-related illness while still living with his partner in Brixton.

There are not many representations of Black Queer figures in British museums. However, in the National Portrait Gallery, there are vintage pictures mostly from 1946 to 1950 of the little-known Jamaican-born Wilbert Passerly, commonly known as Berto Pasuka (1911–63). Pasuka studied classical ballet in Kingston, Jamaica, where he witnessed the descendants of slaves, very likely maroons, dancing to the beat of a drum. Pasuka wanted to share this dance form with wider and new audiences and so moved to London in 1939. Pasuka enrolled at the Astafieva dance school and trained as a dancer and choreographer. Part of Pasuka's interest in dance was also motivated by Marcus Garvey's plans to have a spectacular show that would celebrate the opening of an amusement park in Kingston. Working with Nigerian drummers and other dancers from ethnically mixed backgrounds, Pasuka set up a dance company of his own alongside Ritchie Riley, a fellow Jamaican, which served as a way to express human emotion and explore the contours of Black Queer life. Les Ballets Nègres was Europe's first Black dance company, founded in 1946.

The demonizing of our sexualities and our racial identity has a profound effect upon our bodies. This is something that each of the people named above knew in one way or the other, and this erasure and subjugation was surely a driving force in their work and their creativity. That there are real consequences to the theological language of the Church cannot be contested. What the Church as an institution says about LGBTQ+ people, and its silences around race, really affects actual people. Its speech and its silence lead to suicide, mental health issues, low self-esteem, social isolation and spiritual dilemma. This language renders us 'different' from what is perceived within Christianity as the norm, but the effects of being felt to be abnormal are rarely seen by the Church, and the broken pieces of those the Church has harmed are rarely put back together with the Church's help. Just when we might expect the tender love of Jesus to be put into action in the world by those who claim to follow him, we so often see the opposite in institutional Christianity.

When Pat Califia writes that 'Drug abuse is a gay issue because drugs work even better than orgasms to ease the pain of being different',[44] I hear a call to the Church to recognize that its language lands upon us in such a way that it moves us to seek, by whatever means necessary, ways to nullify the effects of its violent language upon us. It is hard for me to ignore the way in which the ecclesial language, Roman Catholic ecclesial language in particular, rests upon Black Queer bodies, particularly the bodies of those who do not survive the prejudice and discrimination they experience. The Catechism of the Catholic Church states in relation to homosexuality, that:

> Homosexuality refers to relations between men or between women who experience an exclusive or predominant sexual attraction toward persons of the same sex. It has taken a great variety of forms through the centuries and in different cultures. Its psychological genesis remains largely unexplained. Basing itself on Sacred Scripture, which presents homosexual acts as acts of grave depravity, tradition has always declared that 'homosexual acts are intrinsically disordered.' They are contrary to the natural law. They close the sexual act to the gift of life. They do not proceed from a genuine affective and sexual complementarity. Under no circumstances can they be approved.[45]

Despite the many good things that the Pope has said regarding LGBTQ+ life, the official position of the Church has not changed. It is important to state this, and to interrogate whose bodies are included in the community of the Church, and which bodies and whose sexual love are considered to be not just sinful but 'depraved' and 'intrinsically disordered'. If the grace of God does not touch every(body) within the Black Queer community, it touches no one. Those Black Queer bodies cannot wait for any eschatological hope to manifest itself – but need to know here and now that their flesh and story are sacred because we are of God. Every act of Christian worship and every Christian community should question whether it makes that clear. Do All Black Lives Matter here, and do our lives matter before we become bodies? Those on both sides of the sexuality debate might ponder more deeply what the wounds of Christ truly signify. At the cross, our understanding of grace is transformed and our imaginations challenged. At the cross, there is the potential for a new church which, like that body, is deeply wounded but which, in gazing upon the gracious Saviour in the practice of love, might draw all people to itself, becoming in the process a 'fresh creation', thus transformed in order to transform. In embracing its own brokenness with the determination to be made whole, the Church might rediscover itself in and through the very bodies it has so far rejected, in whose body is the Body of Christ. And this work can only be enabled by God – Father, Son and Holy Spirit – who offers grace, of a queer and inclusive kind, of which there is, queerfully, enough for all, for each, and for ever.

The Church, if it is to be the Church, must be the revelation of that divine Love which God 'poured out into our hearts'. Without this love nothing is 'valid' in the Church because nothing is possible. Love alone creates and transforms.[46]

Notes

1 Toni Morrison, *Beloved*, London: Vintage, 2007, p. 89.

2 Phillis Sheppard, *Self, Culture and Others in Womanist Practical Theology*, New York: Palgrave Macmillan, 2011, p. 145.

3 Paul J. Griffiths, *Christian Flesh*, Stanford: Stanford University Press, 2018, p. 1.

4 Lola Olufemi, *Feminism Interrupted: Disrupting Power*, London: Pluto Press, 2020, p. 49.

5 Ibid., p. 51.

6 www.buzzfeed.com/patrickstrudwick/how-many-intersex-chil dren-being-operated-on, accessed 18.3.21.

7 Ibid.

8 Sean Saifa Wall, in Bklyn Boihood, Morgan Mann Willis (ed.), *Outside the XY: Queer Black and Brown Masculinity*, New York: Riverdale Avenue Books, 2016, pp. 145–6.

9 https://lgballiance.org.uk/about/, accessed 18.3.21

10 Olufemi, Feminism Interrupted, p. 60.

11 Linn Marie Tonstad, *Queer Theology: Beyond Apologetics*, Eugene: Cascade Books, 2018. p. 31.

12 Kelly Brown Douglas, *Black Bodies and the Black Church*, New York: Palgrave Macmillan, 2012, p. 183.

13 https://theconversation.com/evangelical-women-are-shaping-public-attitudes-about-sex-work-89129, accessed 18.3.21.

14 Angela Davis, *Freedom is a Constant Struggle: Ferguson, Palestine, and the Foundations of a Movement*, Chicago: Haymarket Books, 2016.

15 M. Shawn Copeland, *Enfleshing Freedom: Body, Race, and Being*, Minneapolis: Fortress Press, 2010, p. 83.

16 Marty Haugen, 'Let us build a House where love can dwell', *Singing the Faith* (409), London: The Methodist Church, 1994.

17 Rowan Williams, 'The Body's Grace', in Charles Hefling (ed.), *Our Selves, Our Souls and Bodies: Sexuality and the Household of God*, Boston: Cowley Press, 1996, p. 59.

18 Terrence Real, *How Can I Get Through To You? Closing the Intimacy Gap*, New York: Simon and Schuster, 2003.

19 C. Beardsley and M. O'Brien, *This is My Body*, London: Darton, Longman & Todd, 2016, p. 60.

20 bell hooks, *Rock My Soul: Black People and Self-Esteem*, New York: Washington Square Press, 2003, pp. 109–10.

21 Barbara Glasson, *A Spirituality of Survival: Enabling a Response to Trauma and Abuse*, London: Continuum, 2009, p. 143.

22 https://aeon.co/essays/black-queer-born-again-a-life-in-and-out-of-the-church, accessed 18.03.21.

23 Douglas, *Black Bodies and the Black Church*, p. 172.

24 Ta-Nehisi Coates, *Between the World and Me*, Melbourne, The Text Publishing Co., 2015.

25 www.churchofengland.org/news-and-media/news-and-statements/new-task-force-ensure-action-over-racism-church-england, accessed 18.03.21.

26 Terrence Real, in bell hooks, *We Real Cool: Black Men and Masculinity*, New York: Routledge, 2004.

27 See my previous work on the history of the Church's role in slavery: www.theschooloftheology.org/posts/essay/why-should-christians-care-slavery-reparations, accessed 18.03.21.

28 JJ Bola, *Mask Off: Masculinity Redefined*, London: Pluto Books, 2019, p. 83.

29 Patrick Califia, *Public Sex: The Culture of Radical Sex*, San Francisco: Cleis Press, 2000, p. xii.

30 www.theguardian.com/commentisfree/2020/oct/09/black-history-month-stories-queer-britain, accessed 18.03.21.

31 Vicky Powell, 'Suicide Note Increases Speculation over Death of Justin Fashanu', *Gay Times* 237, June 1998.

32 http://news.bbc.co.uk/1/hi/uk/167715.stm, accessed 18.03.21.

33 www.washingtonpost.com/archive/local/1998/05/04/soccer-star-accused-of-sex-crime-found-dead/0f14bc04-0cb0-4369-99be-30ab8c4eb994/, accessed 18.03.21.

34 www.youtube.com/watch?v=W7W9CJxRUAY, accessed 18.03.21.

35 https://attitude.co.uk/article/how-homophobia-claimed-the-life-and-career-of-justin-fashanu-the-worlds-first-openly-gay-footballer-1/23928/, accessed 18.03.21.

36 Ibid.

37 https://morningstaronline.co.uk/a-0a28-a-queer-black-life-1, accessed 18.03.21.

38 Gemma Romain, *Race, Sexuality, and Identity in Britain and Jamaica*, London: Bloomsbury, 2017, p. 89.

39 Bernadine Evaristo, *Girl, Woman, Other*, London: Penguin Books, 2019, p. 20.

40 Matt Cook, 'Capital Stories: Local Lives in Queer London', in Jennifer V. Evans and Matt Cook (eds), *Queer Cities, Queer Cultures: Europe since 1945*, London: Bloomsbury Publishing, 2014, p. 47.

41 www.tate.org.uk/tate-etc/issue-44-autumn-2018/portfolio-rotimi-fani-kayode-desire-exile-mark-sealy, accessed 18.03.21.

42 Ibid.

43 Fani-Kayode Rotimi, 'Traces of Ecstasy', *Ten-8*, no. 28, 1988.

44 Califia, *Public Sex*, p. 48.

45 www.vatican.va/archive/ccc_css/archive/catechism/p3s2c2a6.htm, para. 2357, accessed 23.3.21.

46 Alexander Schmemann, *For the Life of the World*, New York: St Vladimir's Seminary Press, 1973, pp. 36–7.

Ecclesiam

She must learn to speak,
Or she must learn to die.
She must learn to weep,
Or she must learn to lie.

She must learn to bleed,
Or she must cause bleeding.
She must find her voice again,
Or she must kill through silence.

There is no other voice that
Can speak her sacred worth
In words.
In signs.
In ritual power.

The Church.

J. R. B.

5

'I'm tired of this Church!'

We humans are free only to be what we are: bearers of the
divine image. Everything else is bondage ...

Wendy Farley[1]

The Church is not above critique. And part of what it means
to exist as those who are Black and LGBTQ+ in the Church is
that our existence in Christian spaces comes with the work of
deconstructing a faith that has been built around our bodily
and spiritual exclusion. That Christianity has existed in Africa
since at least AD 62 means, from where I sit, that as Black
LGBTQ+ people criticisms of the Church are criticisms of a
faith to which we as people have contributed since the very
beginning. In a very real sense, the faith from which we so
often feel and experience brutal exclusion is a faith that is an
ancient part of our story as Black people. Although it is not
the concern of this chapter to address it, the ignorance around
early African Christian history is simply another profound
example of the all-pervasive nature of White Supremacy within
and without the Church, and further adds to the sense of distance we as Black LGBTQ+ people may feel from the Christian
faith. This distortion of history has meant that when the first
missionaries went to Africa to proclaim their version of the
'gospel', they were 'evangelizing' a continent that had already
received orthodox Christianity almost 1800 years earlier. I say
this to make the point that when we tell the Church of our
hurt and disillusionment, when we speak the truth of its treatment of those of us who are Black and LGBTQ+, when we
challenge its doctrines and its theologies, we do so not as med-
dling outsiders but as those to whom the gospel in its earliest
days came, those whose descendants formulated its best
teachings, and those whose Christian roots extend far beyond

missionary activity from England. The concern of this chapter is the nature of the Church and the future of the Church. What constitutes the Church's life, and what might redeem it from itself for the future ... those of us who suffer within it know that the Church is in trouble – not because we say that it is, but because it knows what it needs to do and refuses to do it. The Methodist theologian Leslie Weatherhead remarked in 1965:

> The life of Jesus was a translation into humanity, of the life of God ... in the same way, the Church is not something born on earth which grew to divine proportions and significance, but a translation into terms of space and time of the divine community eternally existent in heaven.[2]

If we wish to speak about the Church as a place of welcome, love, inclusion and therefore true worship, we are forced to think about its life not in the divine sense of it being a mystical body, nor as we hope for it to be, but as it is here on earth. Beyond any notion of the Church as an institution is the basic idea, the image, of the Church as a people, a flock, a community, a body. As a body, as a flock, as community it is conceived from its earliest days of being made up of many and varied parts. St Paul speaks of this in Corinthians when he says:

> For just as the body is one and has many members, and all the members of the body, though many, are one body, so it is with Christ. For in the one Spirit we were all baptized into one body – Jews or Greeks, slaves or free – and we were all made to drink of one Spirit. (1 Corinthians 12.12–13)

> As it is, there are many members, yet one body. The eye cannot say to the hand, 'I have no need of you', nor again the head to the feet, 'I have no need of you.' ... If one member suffers, all suffer together with it; if one member is honoured, all rejoice together with it. Now you are the body of Christ and individually members of it. (1 Corinthians 12.20–21, 26–27)

The chasm between the Church as it is and the Church as it might be is evident to those of us whose breath is stifled by its knee, and who exist as those beyond its body. To us the sickness of the body is evident, and the determination of the Church as a poorly patient adamantly rejecting the very treatment that would make it well is harrowing. The antidote to the body's sickness, of which the famine of grace is a serious symptom, is of course Jesus Christ. Jesus Christ is the Church's only reality, its only hope, its only message. Apart from Jesus Christ crucified, risen and ascended, the Church loses its essence, its message and its heart. In this sense the only real threat to the Church is the Church. Wherever the word 'Church' is used, it ought to be referring to that body, that community, those individuals – broken, sanctified, poured out within which and among whom Jesus and his gospel of radically inclusive love are sovereign. To say this is to say that where this is not the case any reference to the 'Church' is not a reference to the actual Body of Christ, but that which points to where there is in fact no Church at all. That where people are expendable, so too is Christ and his gospel. Wherever we refer to the Church, we should always consider the conduct of that body in the life not of itself but of the world. And this is important, because most of us 'meet' Jesus, or an image of him, when we first encounter the Church – and our convictions about Christian faith can only be those convictions about which our experience of Christian fellowship can make us sure.

For the Church to be the Church it must accept that the gospel it proclaims, that the message with which it seeks to address the world, is one addressed not to faceless masses but to its own broken and disordered life. The Church must allow the awful, awesome, intense reality of God to confront every area of its life, its systems, its conduct. It must, like any of us who know what it means to be born again, hear the message of the gospel as if for the very first time. Because the invitation to follow Jesus Christ is an invitation to live in the deepest Truth, the deepest reality – and in that living we discover that we are not what we pretend we are, but that we are loved just *as* we are. And it is also in that living, as loved and flawed, that we can, in surrender to the Truth that seeks us, become all that we can be. Jesus, for the Church to truly be the Church, must always be more than an idea – Jesus is the living life of God without whom the lungs of the body cannot function, without whom the Church cannot breathe. The relationship of the Church to Jesus is so crucial that the only guarantee of its authenticity is in the degree to which it models its life on his life, the degree to which it loves as he loves, the degree to which, like Christ, it lays down its powerful life for the life of the world to come.

Those who are keen to preserve it as it is are not in fact keen to preserve the Church at all, but that which has become itself a world in which God in Christ cannot find a home, because God in Christ is always an eternal threat to the status quo. And any status quo will be upheld by those who are its direct bene-ficiaries. Pope Paul VI said in a document about evangelism and the Church that the Church begins to evangelize, to share the good news, only once it has itself been converted.[3] And in a sense, the demand our Black LGBTQ+ bodies make upon the Church, because our physical bodies are constrained in social bodies, is simply that the Church become more like its Lord.

One of the difficulties the Church faces is that it can never be the source of its own renewal, however. If it is to thrive as an inclusive community it will do so not because of any programme, initiative or scheme but only because of Jesus Christ. It is its deep knowledge of being founded upon and filled by Jesus Christ alone that gives it the courage to trans-gress its borders. It is Jesus, alive at the heart of the Church, broken and tossed by the winds of its own storm, that moti-vates the Church polity towards that which seeks and saves the marginalized not from themselves but from the brutality and corruption of the world. Jesus is the motivation for all the good the Church might do in the world. Like a lighthouse in the midst of a raging sea, Jesus is the only light that can draw the Church into safe harbour. If the Church proclaimed Jesus, it would have more grace to share for Black LGBTQ+ people and a clearer judgement for the systems, institutions and practices that oppress us even within its own walls. One of the notable differences I find between my own theological outlook and those of many Christians in conservative circles is that, whereas they see the world as the place where 'godless-ness', sin and disorder are situated, I see the Church as the site where these things are right at home. Part of the problem is the reluctance of many Christians to shift their gaze.

As we've seen throughout, to talk of grace is to talk essentially about the character of God. God revealed in Jesus, spoken of by the prophets, proclaimed by the apostles and witnessed to in the martyrs, is free unbounded grace. In giving us grace, God gives Godself in Christ and so God has given Godself to those who are Black and LGBTQ+. It is this given-ness of God that comes to us as complete and unearned gift in Christ. In Christ we see:

> Grace, which asks not a word about what we are, what we have, what we bring along with us; grace, which leaves us no other hope than in that which is undeserved, God's free grace accepts us, just as God's Word has accepted flesh, our flesh. It has accepted us already in Jesus Christ, long before we in turn could think of accepting it. It comforted us already in living and in dying, before we became aware of it, and quite apart from when or how we might have become aware of it.[4]

This grace doesn't ask for our opinion of ourselves, but rather for our opinions of ourselves as God sees us – for God's opinion of us. Grace means the view we have of ourselves should be the view God has of us ... or, in the words of Karl Barth: 'Grace simply wants to have us: to have us as we are in the Church.' If the Church is not there for Black LGBTQ+ people, then it is not there for God.

> If the Church does not love the message of free grace (if it stands apart from the people with too many scruples, if it meets them with too many reproaches), if it is afraid of that message and is too pious and moralistic for people – what is the Church then? Nothing, nothing at all![5]

As romantic as our thinking about the Church might become, and as tempting as it might be to talk about an ideal, it is the Church as it is, and therefore as we as Black LGBTQ+ people have experienced it, that we must most forcefully speak about. If it is true, and I believe it is, that 'Jesus judges our Christian discipleship, and therefore [the Church's ministry] simply in terms of whether or not real human need is met with real human care, compassion and concern',[6] then the Church as it is in many places is failing in this task. This failure is an impediment to the Church's proclamation, as Robert Thompson notes:

> The mission of the Church will be severely inhibited because when the increasing popular perception is that the Church does not uphold either the full dignity of women or of LGBTi (*sic*) people, it will find it progressively more difficult to be heard when it addresses the gospel to other pressing ethical issues of our contemporary life.[7]

In 2018, a video[8] went viral of a 6-year-old Black boy, Nazir Ferrell, from a church service in the United States. In it, Nazir, totally unaware that he was being filmed, is given a microphone as though he'd been pressured into making a speech or giving a testimony. Having given in to the pressure of the saints (the older people of the congregation), Nazir suddenly declares to the gathered people of God in a loud, clear and unapologetic voice the words: 'I'm tired of this Church!' Having said what he said, he thrusts the microphone back into the hands of an adult and, as the congregation gasps in shock, he marches away in a strop and goes right back to his seat. Immediately when I saw this clip, I felt something inside me acknowledge so deeply the truth in the tone of his phrase. Although uttered by a little Black boy of small stature, his words were full of intention, power and meaning. Shared by friends and family, retweeted and posted almost everywhere, we knew precisely what Nazir meant, what he felt and what motivated him to say what he said. We shared it not just because it induced laughter, but also because it resonated with us. In one way or the other, as adults or as children, we know what that feels like. We have all been that young Black child at a church or Christian event – forced into participating in something we just don't really have the energy or time for; yet going along with it anyway because – 'children should be seen and not heard …!'

I stand with Nazir. I'm not tired of the Church, but I am so often tired of *this* Church, lots of us are tired of *this* Church. We're tired of the homophobic, transphobic, misogynistic, heteronormative cowardly embodiment of White Supremacist 'Christianity' and injustice that the Church so often is. I'm tired of having to play along. I'm tired of having the microphone thrust in my face and the gathered people of God sitting there expecting to know the script, because it was already written. What so many of us are tired of isn't even really the Church, rather it is an institution passing for the Church, and if Christianity, as we see it today, was equal to its many proud pretensions, perhaps portions of its institutional life could be redeemed. But now, from where I stand, I am not so sure. As Azariah France-Williams says in his book on institutional racism and the Church of England, 'we cannot wait for the system to dismantle itself. We have to do it ourselves.'[9]

For the sake of what follows in this chapter I will refer to the institutional embodiment of the Christian faith as the 'Church', but I am of the view, perhaps even the conviction now, that our being Church as Jesus Christ may have intended is an aspiration not yet a reality. In other words, I believe that if anything such as a 'church' existed in the mind and heart of Jesus it is yet to come to birth, and does not yet exist. I believe too that those of us within the Church who think that God will somehow make *this* Church better are deluded, because God's blessing cannot be outpoured upon a church that does not exist. Somehow the 'Church' of Jesus Christ, in its present embodiment, must acknowledge how far it is from the kind of community its Lord would recognize as rightfully bearing his name. Only a church that gives its life for the poor and the suffering, only a church that feeds the hungry and clothes the naked, only a church that goes out in search of the lost and exiled, the trans and gay, Black and Queer, can truly be the Church of Jesus Christ. Until it does so, it is living as an illegitimate child, seeking to bring others into a family that it itself does not belong to. What Nazir knew, we all know deep down. That whatever Jesus had in mind for his disciples' future, this isn't quite it. That the economy of God where grace flows freely isn't the economy the Church is operating within.

That our structures are our strictures, and our gospel only a half-gospel, preaching grace and redemption to those who are already within our walls and condemnation to those who are LGBTQ+ beyond them.

The Church, then, if it is to be the Church of Jesus, must stop clothing itself in the aesthetics of liberation and re-commit itself to the labour of that love of God that is both revolutionary and inclusive – this work is occasionally offensive to those who wish to withhold power, and shocking to those whose only way towards progress is one of civility and respectability. Justice work, love work, is troubling work. To do all this, the work that is the labour of love, we have to look hard at the Church as it is, and look hard to Jesus Christ as he was revealed to us, not as he has been presented to us through the lens and filter of Whiteness. In doing this, in looking again at itself and again at the Jesus revealed in history and active in the present, the Church can renew, perhaps, its theology as itself a disciple of Christ. Having done this, it can itself become, perhaps, a vehicle for the liberative love of God in the world for all people, including Black LGBTQ+ people.

A converted Church would recognize that any Christian theology that neglects to take up the cause of the oppressed, the lesbian, the gay, the bisexual, the trans, and all God's children as central to its contemplation of God is a theology in total service of the oppressor. This is, of course, just another way of saying that all Christian theology has to begin with a contemplation of God as God has been revealed ... as God has revealed Godself in the world, and not merely as the Church might imagine or desire. It is the worship of the God of our imaginations, the White imagination, that has led to the famine of grace in the Church. A White God who sends a White Jesus into a White world to save White people through a White Church is a God whose interest is reserved only for the powerful and the comfortable, and who has no good news for the Black and Brown LGBTQ+ poor. This God, along with his Son, must be crucified by the Church if it is ever to worship the Jesus who came to be its life and who made it his body.

So far, two things have been said that might seem quite startling – first, that the Church as Jesus desires it does not exist and, second, that the Church as it is must destroy its White Lord in order to become the Church it can be. What has become abundantly clear in the Church's treatment of Black and LGBTQ+ people is that, more than any other institution, the Church itself needs God. It needs the true and living God, not the god of the White Supremacist imagination, but the foot-washing, crucified, wounded God revealed in the Black Jesus who did not cling to power or earthly glory, but who empowered the downtrodden and persecuted. It is only this God who will motivate and convince the Church as it is to go beyond itself in search of Black and Brown bodies, many of whom are LGBTQ+.

James Baldwin, himself both Black and gay, and a preacher in his youth, had a damning critique of the Christian Church. He noted a distinction between his own Christian tradition and that of White American Christians.

In the Church I come from – which is not at all the same Church to which white Americans belong – we were counselled, from time to time, to do our first works over. Though the Church I come from and the Church to which most white Americans belong are both Christian churches, their relationship – due to those pragmatic decisions concerning Property made by a Christian State sometime ago – cannot be said to involve, or suggest, the fellowship of Christians. We do not, therefore, share the same hope or speak the same language. To do your first works over means to re-examine everything. Go back to where you started, or as far back as you can, examine all of it, travel your road again and tell the truth about it. Sing or shout or testify or keep it to yourself: but know whence you came.[10]

In July 1968, Baldwin was invited to address the World Council of Churches, which was, that particular year, meeting in Uppsala. Choosing the title 'White Racism or World Community?' Baldwin presented the global Church with what I suspect was essentially an ultimatum. Many people forget that the major force that formed and shaped him was the Church. Although evident in almost everything he writes and particularly in his work *Go Tell It on the Mountain*, many folk equate his leaving the pulpit with having left the faith of Jesus Christ. But these are not the same thing. Part of what gives Baldwin's critique of the Church such power is his choice to walk away from it having been so much a part of it. Like Nazir, Baldwin was 'tired of this Church', so much so that he expresses working within it while always being outside of it. We should never doubt the validity of his call to be a preacher in his youth – it wouldn't be the first time the Church had failed to embrace a prophet of God, and I can assure you that Baldwin was not the last. Baldwin was simply not desired by the Church, the same Church that summoned him to impart his wisdom in 1968.

In Uppsala, Baldwin presented himself as 'one of the creatures, one of God's creatures, whom the Christian Church has most betrayed'. In addressing the global Church he both makes an accusation and a plea, a plea that he says was articulated by Jesus Christ himself. For Baldwin, it was a contradiction that the Church expected Black people to see themselves as equal children of God when their experience of the church structures spoke of a different reality. As Black folk, we are told that the culture of Britain and America is essentially 'a Christian culture', yet there was nothing of Christ in the Colonial powers and Colonial impulse that still exists and that captured and brutalized our ancestors.

Central to Baldwin's accusation was the fact that the Jesus the Church presents us with, whom we are told was born in Bethlehem and grew up in Nazareth, comes to us blue-eyed and blonde-haired, such that 'all the virtues to which I, as a Black man, was expected to aspire had, by definition, to be white'. In all of this is a Church that is, in most places, led by White people who are baffled sometimes by the criticism that we as Black people make of the Church and who are reluctant to enter into what being Black in a racist world really means, and why the Church's history, when properly examined, is less than praiseworthy. The Church now 'is in great danger not merely because the Black people say it is but because people are always in great danger when they know what they should do, and refuse to act on that knowledge'. For Baldwin the sickness of the Church is located in its relationship with privilege and power. He says, 'part of the dilemma of the Christian Church is the fact that it opted, in fact, for power and betrayed its own first principles which were a responsibility to every living soul'. Essentially, from where Baldwin and I stand, the Church lives as a body that refuses to hear the commandment, 'Love one another as I have loved you.'

Baldwin really brings things home by mentioning the ways that Stokely Carmichael, a prominent Civil Rights leader, was spoken of as a young, 'very dangerous, radical, Black fanatic racist', but most people, including those within the Church, forget that Stokely Carmichael started life as a Christian,

> doing day by day and hour by hour precisely what the Christian Church is supposed to do, to walk from door to door, to feed the hungry, to speak to those who are oppressed, to try to open the gates of prisons for all those who are imprisoned. And a day came, inevitably, when this young man grew weary of petitioning a heedless population and said, in effect, what all revolutionaries have always said, 'I petitioned you and petitioned you'. And you can petition for a long, long time, but the moment comes when the petitioner is no longer a petitioner, but has become a beggar.[11]

Baldwin knew that he too was like those who came before him, addressing a Church that wasn't taking the message of that rebel preacher from Galilee seriously. The Church was an institution that had rationalized its violent behaviour and absolved itself of all culpability, such that so distant from its crimes and its victims it is no longer in touch with its true self. The Church's own denial of reality induces a kind of falsehood in others. We see slowly that 'the lies the Christian Church has always helplessly told about [us] are only a reflection of the lies the Christian Church has always helplessly told itself, to itself, about itself'.[12] Black Queer Christians who still belong to the Church stand in the midst of it as the sharpest reminder of all the Church seeks to ignore and leaves unaddressed.

It is easy to miss the fact that Baldwin is, in his words here, addressing the World Council of Churches just a couple of months after Dr King was assassinated. For Black people in the USA and beyond, and particularly for Baldwin, King's death marked what felt like a curtain call for racial justice en route to a different world. Not only did King's death have a monumental impact on Baldwin, but it revealed a deep hatred, almost insurmountable in the heart of White America – for what was clear was that even the most Christlike of people could not survive the heat of White racism. Dr King's death was the culmination of the many silences of a complicit White Christianity, and a church that had ignored Dr King's summons and thus distorted the gospel enough to have not only enslaved our ancestors but sought the enslavement of our souls in its preaching of a non-gospel. In his closing words, Baldwin says:

> The Christian Church still rules this world, it still has the power, to change the structure of South Africa. It has the power, if it will, to prevent the death of another Martin Luther King Junior. It has the power, if it will, to force my Government to cease dropping bombs in South-East Asia. These are crimes committed in the name of the Christian Church … if the Christian faith does not recover its Lord and Saviour Jesus Christ, we shall discover the meaning of what he meant when he said, 'Insofar as have done it (*sic*) unto the least of these, you have done it unto me'.[13]

If Baldwin is right, then the question remains – what *is* the Church going to do with its power, and why has it not listened to what was said to it so clearly in 1968?

Part of what many find tiring about the Church is more than just the fact that it isn't what it claims to be, but more fundamentally what we find tiring about this Church is that it has gone so far from what Jesus was and is about. The most unattractive thing about us as a church is that we are not honest, or authentic, or real about who we really are. When we have claimed to be the depository of truth, we have the place in which the truth is most fervently denied. People of course would be forgiven today for not knowing that Jesus wasn't a Scandinavian-looking White man from a middle-class family with enough wealth to create the brand that is Christianity. The Church has done a poor job at getting the true message of Jesus out there. In so many places it has retreated from the public square into the safety of its memberships and its groups, its fellowships and brigades, cafes and crypts. Hidden behind closed doors or websites that are impossible to navigate, those who seek Jesus cannot find him because we hold to the myth that he lives within, and only within, our church communities. Yet Jesus is roaming freely, and his heart yearns to move among Queer folk, not just beside us but as one of us. So who was he and how did he live? Beyond the story of his birth explored in the earlier chapters, how Jesus lived in his adulthood tells us much about his identity too, and also much about the kind of legacy he sought to leave.

At the beginning of his ministry according to Matthew's Gospel, having left Nazareth and made his home in Capernaum, Jesus goes to Galilee for some alone time. As he walked by the sea of Galilee a little later, he sees two fishermen, Peter and Andrew, throwing their nets into the lake. The only credentials Jesus could have known about them were that they were human beings who could fish; we don't know how perfect their fishing technique is, we don't know what kind of people they are, we know nothing about whether they are single or married, straight or gay, scripture doesn't even tell us about their age or physical appearance. But Jesus sees something in them, he calls them to follow him, and they do. Then a little later Jesus sees another two brothers, James and John. Again he knows nothing about them – this time they just happen to be in a boat showing no skills or special qualities except how to manage themselves on the water. Jesus calls them to follow him, and again, they do so – leaving their boat and their father in it, as they follow this Jesus they know nothing about. Thus begins a whole new life, opening on to a whole new world for these four people and Jesus. Their lives are never the same again, as they eventually become a group of 12 and travel around the Mediterranean following this wandering rebel rabbi. While we have little information available to us about the childhood of Jesus, and nothing about his education, teenage years and early adulthood, his entry on to the main stage of life in the Middle East shows us someone whose way was simple and whose interests were clear – his way was one of love, his interests were people and all the things that hurt and oppressed them. But Jesus does not enter the pages of the Gospels without a certain context. Jesus comes to us intimately linked to the character of John the Baptist, that hermit-like Russell Brand type of character who lives in the wilderness by the River Jordan and preaches repentance and renewal to those eagerly expecting the Kingdom of God. In his life, death and resurrection, Jesus points to, preaches and possesses this Kingdom preached also by John. Covered in camel skin and eating just locusts and honey for food, John ushers the adult Jesus on to the gospel pages and presents him to us as a long-expected Messiah. Easy though it is to miss, the Jesus we have enthroned in splendour comes to us as a homeless follower and disciple of this camel-hair-wearing preacher John, and it is John who baptizes Jesus. It is from John the Baptist, and from the prophetic tradition in which Jesus stood, that he gets some of his ideals – the need for repentance in the life of any of us searching for God's Kingdom, the need for justice and kindness in our life together, and the primacy of God's reign in our broken and fragile world. The Jesus of the Gospels is, at his most basic, a charismatic prophet, an image typical of a 'man of God' within the Jewish tradition. He is a Galilean holy man, who, like others, had disciples. Jesus is also an exorcist, healer, itinerant preacher and friend of sinners. As the Gospels tells us, 'he cured many who were sick with various diseases' (Mark 1.34; 3.10), he cleansed lepers (Luke 5.13), forgave sin (Luke 7.48), brought the dead back to life (Luke 8.55), and fed five thousand starving people (Luke 9.17). Time and again we see a Jesus who cares little for the issues of ritual purity of his day, has no concern for his reputation in the eyes of the elite and powerful, and who breaks the common boundaries between the clean and the unclean, those on the inside and those socially and spiritually outcast. Jesus takes the dead by the hand, allows the bleeding to touch his clothes, eats with tax collectors and has his feet washed by 'sinful' women (Luke 7.37). We can have no doubt that Jesus' way of life was intended to be a model for his disciples, and therefore a model for the Church given that he involved them fully in this life, as Mark's Gospel so clearly reveals: 'As he sat at dinner in Levi's house, many tax-collectors and sinners were eating with Jesus and his disciples …' (2.15). As a leader, Jesus embodies vulnerability not only on the cross and in his betrayal but more tenderly as he weeps at the grave of his dead friend Lazarus in what is the shortest verse in the Bible: 'Jesus wept' (John 11.35, NIV). And when he entrusts his mother to his beloved disciple John we read: 'When Jesus saw his mother and the disciple whom he loved standing beside her, he said to his mother, "Woman, here is your son." Then he said to the disciple, "Here is your mother"' (John 19.26–27). Even in death, Jesus is thinking about the welfare of others – ensuring his mother and best friend carry each other through and offering hope to dying thieves on the cross beside him: 'Truly I tell you, today you will be with me in Paradise' (Luke 23.43). Jesus, in life and in death, from birth to ascension, shows a solidarity with people upon whom he poured out his Father's grace. In all of this, Jesus shows no special interest in the fine detail of people's lives; for him the fact that they are human is enough for them to qualify for his loving attention and embrace.

Azariah France-Williams notes: 'The Church should be – could be – a portal to another world where the principles of justice, the person of Jesus, and the philosophy of journey prevails. But it is not.'[14] Rather, the Church has chosen to distance itself from a Jesus who accompanied people through life, with all that entailed and all that would eventually cost him. While Jesus operated like many other holy men and charismatic preachers, his message was unique. His was a love and salvation, a healing and freedom, not just for some but for all. In Matthew's Gospel, Jesus says so clearly: 'Come to me, all you that are weary and are carrying heavy burdens, and I will give you rest' (Matthew 11.28). Given the universality of his love and the basic nature of his message, it has always been a source of discomfort to me that this simple way of the carpenter of Nazareth who calls people to follow him without inquiring into their worthiness has become so complicated, so fraught with terms and conditions, so laced with hoops through which a potential Christian must jump that it seems to me no longer related to that communal way of love that Jesus started. This Jesus proclaimed a Kingdom not beyond people's reach, nor one that they had to wait to be dead in order to live in, instead

Jesus proclaimed that 'The Kingdom of God is in the midst of you' (Luke 17.20, ESV). All that Jesus came to do, and all that his ministry is about, is guiding his disciples (us) to the Kingdom he so often spoke of where justice and peace and equality reign. In his preaching, though, Jesus reverses the priorities of the tradition he stands in. For Jesus it is the poor, the widow, the orphan, the prisoner and the sick who are at the forefront of his mind and his message such that he makes little appeal to those who are righteous, whose lives appear 'sorted', but instead directs his attention and his preaching to the lost sheep to whom he is nothing but a loving and compassionate shepherd – one who lays down his life for the sheep who wander and go astray. The minister, philosopher and civil rights activist Howard Thurman touches on how distant the Christianity of our day has become from Christ's own faith:

> The basic fact is that Christianity as it was born in the mind of this Jewish teacher and thinker appears as a technique of survival for the oppressed. That it became, through the intervening years, a religion of the powerful and the dominant, used sometimes as an instrument of oppression, must not tempt us into believing that it was thus in the mind and life of Jesus. 'In him was life; and the life was the light of men.' Wherever his spirit appears, the oppressed gather fresh courage; for he announced the good news that fear, hypocrisy, and hatred, the three hounds of hell that track the trail of the disinherited, need have no dominion over them.[15]

Jesus knew intimately the relationship between the people he lived among and the power and violence of the Roman Empire that at one time eventually took his life. Jesus had alternative models of leadership, alternative models of power and alternative models of masculinity all around him – yet he chose to model servant kingship, he chose to be a wounded healer, and he chose to be the friend of sinners, a companion and confidant to men and women in a patriarchal society. Jesus understood the anatomy of human relationships to such an extent that he knows and displays the understanding that love is the foundation of all trust. When, in the same text, Howard Thurman

says, 'I belong to a generation that finds very little that is meaningful or intelligent in the teachings of the Church', he seems
to have echoed something that rings true still today for many.
Although we find God in the shape of Christ who lives as the
proximity of God to us in the midst of our fragile world, this
disconnect between the Church and the people of our day is, I
believe, rooted in the Church's betrayal of the movement Jesus
began, and its portrayal of someone we fail to recognize as
God. The Church at its highest level and leadership simply has
no idea of the real lives that we as Black LGBTQ+ people live.
It has distanced itself from our reality, and we do not see ourselves within it at almost any level. This disconnect affects the
way we who are Black and LGBTQ+ relate to the gospel. The
Jesus we hear proclaimed by the Church relates to us neither
through our Black experiences of the world nor through our
Queer identities, and the gospel we are presented with is one
that so often demands of us that we leave our bodies, and our
politics, outside our worship. The Christ who called people
to follow him as they are calls us (in the Church's language)
to follow him only once we have given up our Blackness and
become straight and White. The Christ offered to us is one
who can save every part of us, but who it appears is adamant
that our sexuality cannot be held or embraced by him as that
which is wholesome and holy and valued. And it is a strange
thing, that this Jesus who is so Queer to us, whom we know
so deeply in the depths of our hearts to be at work among
us and our love, is said to be incapable of loving us in the
deepest and most passionate way. Anyone under any doubt as
to whether or not Jesus loves people as they are should take
another look at the Jesus we see in the Gospels. In them, we see
a Jesus who lives essentially as a man of the people. Jesus, as
a working man, spends all his days among the poor, where he
was both known and loved because he knew and loved them.
He lived his life among the crowd to the extent that Matthew
tells us: 'When [Jesus] saw the crowds, he had compassion
for them, because they were harassed and helpless, like sheep
without a shepherd' (Matthew 9.36). None of us can claim to
be a disciple of this wounded and risen sun-kissed man from
Nazareth unless we too love the poor and can name them.

When Alfred Lord Tennyson wrote in 1855 that 'the Churches have killed their Christ' he touches on what is at root when grace is in famine. Yet, the Church has not killed its Christ; in fact it has given birth to a Christ who is almost entirely mythical. Our Christ, the White Christ, has no interest in the poor – he is not surrounded by a weak and sinful multitude, instead we have crowned and enthroned him, robed him in earthly glory and placed him so high in our constructs of heaven that he is beyond reach and of no earthly use to those who suffer at the hands of men who look just like him and uphold the same systems. If the Church is to become the Body of Christ, one of its earliest priorities must be to fall in love (perhaps for the very first time) with the people Jesus loves, and to love them like he loves them. That means all people, without reserve, and not excluding the Black LGBTQ+ children of God. This call to a simplicity in the practice of love is no small task for the people of God who call themselves Christian. It asks the Church to see the world as the place where God in Christ is already at work, and to follow that God in all the places Jesus would go. The Church, even as it is, 'with all its failings and its yearnings, has to learn how to persist in its task in the world',[16] even if that task asks for the sacrifice of its own life.

In my early days of discerning a vocation to priesthood, I was privileged to be in correspondence with the Revd Dr Kenneth Greet, who in a few handwritten letters would encourage me to keep listening to the voice of God that I felt drawing me towards ordination. Kenneth's work touches so often on the social evils of his day, particularly racism and what is often called 'issues' of human sexuality. On the Church's relationship to the gospel, Kenneth Greet said:

> Those who dismiss what they call 'the social gospel' in favour of the gospel of personal salvation are making a division where none exists, nor can exist. There are not two gospels, but one. The gospel is both personal and social.[17]

In living out that gospel,

> The Christian faith asserts that this social God who is invisible was made incarnate in Jesus Christ. The Church exists

to mirror that image. This it can do only as it shows forth in its own life and seeks to create in the life of the world that perfect unity in diversity which is the hallmark of the character of the God whom Christians worship. In a world broken and fragmented by sin, the Church, if it is true to its mission, cannot be other than an agent of revolution. The greatest safeguard against the threat of often dangerous half-truths, is wholehearted devotion to Jesus Christ and the truth of His everlasting Gospel.

To a church that has fallen deaf to the cry of Black LGBTQ+ people, to a church that is gripped by racism, homophobia and transphobia, to a church that exists in ultimate service of the powerful, Kenneth Greet's words still bear a prophetic witness, a witness to a church in which grace is in famine: 'A Church that fails to hear that cry (the cry for justice and for action) is [a Church] deaf to the voice of God, and that deafness is fatal.'[18] There is a death-ness in the Church today of which those of us who have been pushed towards the door know and have diagnosed for some time. It is a diagnosis rooted in both the cowardice of the Church as an institution and its crisis of identity. While it has been busy telling LGBTQ+ people what to do with their desire, and telling its Black members how to express their anger, it has lost its desire for the one thing that matters: God, and God's children.

The faith of the Church, what it is that the Church claims to believe – its true DNA and identity – is summed up in its creeds, its statements of belief. In the Nicene Creed, developed at a council of the Church in AD 325, we find two words, which although rushed over when we say them, are so important to think about. These two simple words are speaking about God and the motivation behind God's action in the world. The words are 'for us'. And they come before the words:

and for our salvation came down from heaven,
And was incarnate by the Holy Ghost of the Virgin Mary,
And was made man,
And was crucified also *for us* under Pontius Pilate.

Only twice in the Creed do we hear the words 'for us', and they sum up and spell out something very special about our Black LGBTQ+ lives. That it is *for us* that Christ came and *for us* that Christ died. *For us* that he bore his burden, *for us* that he suffered, *for us* that he came to pour out his grace, make known his love and give his peace. Jesus, in sharing our life, enables us to share the life he has with the Father and in doing so ushers in the age of grace, *for us*. In God there is no famine, just abundant love – for all, for ever. In the words of Fred Pratt Green's hymn:

> *He came to share temptation,*
> *our utmost woe and loss;*
> *for us and our salvation*
> *to die upon the cross.*
> *So, when the Dove descended*
> *on him, the Son of Man,*
> *the hidden years had ended,*
> *the age of grace began.*[19]

The White Jesus, however, can never be for us, and can never exist where grace is abundant. This is why he is so at home in the Church as it is. The White Jesus of capitalism, patriarchy, misogyny, White Supremacy, homophobia and transphobia is a Jesus founded upon and fashioned out of all of the things that Jesus did *not* do, neither in history nor in scripture – only in the White imagination. The White Church and the Black Churches that have married into Whiteness must be reminded that 'no dogma, religious principle, or experience deserves to be privileged over history'.[20] It is the task, then, of Black historians, Black theologians, Womanist scholars and Queer theologians who are serious about radical liberation and inclusion to make the sun-kissed Jewish Jesus visible. Whenever the Church is complacent with White representations of Jesus and liturgical language that demonizes Blackness, liking it to sin and evil, it willingly partakes in the sin of racism and excludes all bodies that are not White, non-disabled, cis-gendered and powerful. It is the vocation of the Church to recognize:

The sin of man [sic] asserts itself in racial pride, racial hatreds and persecutions, and in the exploitations of other races. Against this in all its forms the Church is called by God to set its face implacably and to utter its word inequivocally [sic], both within and without its own borders. Moreover it is the first responsibility of the Church to demonstrate within its own fellowship the reality of community as God intends it.[21]

As a young Black Queer leader in the Church, it has concerned me greatly how few of the young Christians I know look like me or share my background. The Church has rendered itself almost invisible and irrelevant to many young Black people, especially those who are LGBTQ+. At my grandmother's funeral, as we lowered her coffin into the ground, we sang some traditional Jamaican graveside hymns. The irony of these songs being considered 'Jamaican' is that they were written by the blind and prolific hymn-writer Fanny Crosby, who was a White woman. Still, they have entered the Jamaican repertoire and have stuck. As I led the singing, I noticed that apart from the older folk, my aunts and uncles and older cousins, the singing stopped at my sister and me in terms of age. Our younger cousins, who came after me (I was the youngest for many years), didn't know the words, didn't get what we were doing, and didn't seem to understand its significance. As I looked at their faces, I suddenly realized that not only was the connection between the ground upon which we stood and Jamaican soil growing ever thinner, but the connection between their generation and the Church's grammar was passing away too. As we sang about 'marching to Zion', and of our soon and very soon 'grand time up in heaven', and as we sang of 'the glorious gift of His love' and of 'that bright and cloudless morning when the dead in Christ shall rise' I knew that neither the words nor the movement of our spirits made sense to them – they did not know why we sang, or why we stood there filling in a grave both weeping and rejoicing. As the descendants of those enslaved, standing at the grave of our beloved departed and singing the words of resurrection hope has profound meaning. Some of this is hidden in the deep paradox of other words also sung, like 'No more cold iron shackles on my feet' and 'Let us labour for the Master from the dawn till setting sun' – these lose all their bittersweet remembrances in the minds of those who are taught neither their history nor a relevant Christianity. It made me wonder, will they ever know the deep truth of Jesus and his gospel that enabled so many of the Windrush generation and our closest ancestors to close their eyes on the world filled with the hope that they would one day see the Lord?

> *Oh, the soul thrilling rapture when I view His blessed face,*
> *And the luster of His kindly beaming eye;*
> *How my full heart will praise Him for the mercy, love*
> *and grace*
> *That prepared for me a mansion in the sky.*[22]

With Churches such as SPAC Nation[23] (currently being investigated over financial and safeguarding concerns[24]) utilizing the poverty of young Black people in their preaching of a gospel of prosperity, the famine of grace becomes clothed in false abundance. In this version of Christianity there are no 'mansions in the sky', just opulence here on earth – because wealth is seen as a symbol of God's blessing. Professor Anthony Reddie, writing on the relationship between Black Churches and Whiteness, notes:

> While British Pentecostalism provides the emotional and liturgical cathartic space in which the Black self can seek repose in experiential worship and African and Caribbean religio-cultural aesthetics, the theological underpinning in such settings remains studiously wedded to White Euro-American fundamentalism.[25]

The popularity of a group like SPAC Nation (Salvation Proclaimers Anointed Church) does show us one thing in relation to the spaces Black Christians of a certain generation and background seek. It shows us that young Black people are hungry for the gospel, and that some Christian organizations are attempting (poorly) to fill gaps that others have abandoned. In their searching, these young Black folk often put themselves at great risk, often in conservative Christian spaces in which openly LGBTQ+ people would most certainly not find a home. The African American writer, feminist and social activist bell hooks writes about how this sense of spiritual longing within many Black people is often abused and capitalized upon. She says:

> When soulfulness gets turned into just another commodity to be bought and sold in the market-place, its power to transform lives is diminished ... Black capitalists have been just as eager and as willing as their White counterparts to destroy the soulfulness that sustains life and replace it with a shallow sense of soul that makes material gain the only major signifier of progress.[26]

There is an entire generation of young folk, many of whom are young Black folk who have within them a burning desire for the deep, rich, fulfilling spiritual life that Jesus offers. Many of these young people are LGBTQ+ and have yet to see a church that can welcome them as they are, and journey with them through the highs and lows, the joys and griefs of this life – this absence, this lack of welcome, has meant that their deep and real spiritual longing is easily monopolized by those who have no sense of pastoral duty towards them, and for whom the gospel has absolutely no real meaning or value. This means that there is a real urgency for the Church, which considers itself to be Christ's body on earth, to be that body for all of God's children and not just a select few. While 'Black Christianity in the wake of the Windrush Generation has offered either implicit or explicit models of Black self-affirmation and identity in the continuing struggle against racism and White Supremacy in the British context,'[27] it has failed in offering affirmation to Black LGBTQ+ individuals.

If the Church of Jesus Christ has inherited the gift of the gospel, then this must be its most supreme treasure, because the gospel is the good news of the Saviour who came to seek and save the lost and who gave his very life for the Church and the world. It is the Church's responsibility to live and preach this good news to the world, and it ought to feel like good news when it is heard! It is a gospel that has a world-transforming intimacy at its heart, a gospel that tells the story of a diverse people gathered around a Queer God – three in one – embodied in the beloved, Jesus Christ. That Jesus left behind a group of believers who lived as revolutionaries at the heart of a relentlessly powerful Roman Empire should not be overlooked. These disciples offered the kind of alternative community that we so desperately need to see more of in our world today.

While the Roman Empire carried out its business through the use of brute force and by the sword, the early Church shaped its life differently. The early Christian community was marked by its hope, its inclusivity and its togetherness, for it was the place where 'All who believed were together and had all things in common; they would sell their possessions and goods and distribute the proceeds to all, as any had need' (Acts 2.44–45). This is a far cry from the Rolls Royce-driving pastors of independent Churches, and miles away from a 'get rich or die trying' gospel! It is about this early church community that Jesus prayed, 'that they may all be one. As you, Father, are in me and I am in you, may they also be in us, so that the world may believe …' (John 17.21), and in this community that the Spirit intercedes for the whole people of God with sighs too deep for words (Romans 8.26–27). It is in the Christian community, this basic microcosm of God's plan for humanity, that we learn that we are more than the abuses we have suffered, but rather conquerors, that we can live as those 'convinced that neither death, nor life, nor angels, nor rulers, nor things present, nor things to come, nor powers, nor height, nor depth, nor anything else in all creation, will be able to separate us from the love of God in Christ Jesus our Lord' (Romans 8.38–39). The Church of today, however, has subjugated grace into the realm of discourse, such that we speak about grace but rarely see it embodied, and we, if we are LGBTQ+, are people about whom the Church in many places is still making its mind up. If the Church is the place where revolutionary love and intimacy can exist, it must become the place in which both love and desire are at the centre and its own body as the Body of Christ must be porous and open to us and all that we are. We are the Church. The myth of our separated-ness might lead us to believe that we truly are beyond it, but we, Black LGBTQ+ and Christian, are members of it. Since we constitute its life we are part of its body.

> If my sister or brother is not at the table, we are not the flesh of Christ. If my sister's mark of sexuality must be obscured, if my brother's mark of race must be disguised, if my sister's mark of culture must be repressed, then we are not the flesh of Christ. For, it is through and in Christ's own flesh that the 'other' is my sister, is my brother; indeed, the 'other' is me.[28]

In a sermon preached at Hope College in 2014, the Revd Professor Willie James Jennings said regarding the Church that it has not yet

> grasped the importance of desire for God. We still function as though desire is something God wants to destroy or at least imprison. We have not yet come to realize that desire is the currency that flows through the new that God has done and is doing in this world. I am convinced that the future of the church will be found only in the places and spaces where people have learned to desire one another, and out of that desire to care for one another, and stand together against the forces of death. Yes, multi-racial, yes, multi-cultural, yes people of every orientation, but fundamentally people who have found their way to love through desire. They are together not because they have to be together, not because they are bound by some ethic or principle, but because they want to be together.[29]

If desire is the thing that pushes the Church towards its future, we have to imagine what kind of work can take the Church to the place where we can say to one another without fear or trembling, or particularly have it said to us as those who are Black and LGBTQ+, 'I desire you, beloved in Christ, my sibling and kin ... and, I desire to care for you, beloved, just as you are, in this Church which is itself, to many – perhaps especially to you, a force of death.'

What would it take to create a church where those who consider themselves our allies, and those who have the potential to become our allies, look us in the eye and say these words? Perhaps we do not consider enough just how much work it will take for a church that has demonized desire, particularly LGBTQ+ desire, to begin to foster desire – a desire that, as the very desire of God enables us, whoever we are, to desire one another as God desires us? If this work of desire is too much like hard work, then perhaps we must abolish the Church. A church that cannot commit to radical, inclusive, love in action is a church that I believe must be abolished. As the feminist systematic theologian Sarah Coakley has said, 'churches need to be more radically destabilized by the challenge that the Holy Spirit presses upon us',[30] and the biggest challenge we find in the Church at the moment is in its inability to unequivocally love LGBTQ+ people, as well as in its inability to do deep and meaningful anti-racist work. This destabilization, which I believe may already be occurring, leads me to see that the only remedy for the Church's mess is its own destabilization, its own de(con)struction. When I say, then, that the Church must be abolished, I mean no harm to the message of Jesus or the man himself – I love both, and preach both. By abolition, I seek to return both to the person and to the message. When I say that the Church must be abolished, I mean the total and complete dismantling of the White Christian project, which is not a church but a club, failing in both holiness and welcome, which is found worshipping, faithfully, a heap of ashes at the altar of Empire. This abolition, in the British context, would certainly mean that the Church must sever all ties and privileges that come with being 'Established', or respectable – or at the very least that the Establishment and its privileges need to be redefined. Yet even here, I have to ask why any of us who've seen the true face of these institutions should be committed to a belief in its ability to reform itself when, after so many centuries, it has chosen not to. It is not reform the Church needs, rather it needs to be born again, brought to its knees before its Lord. When I say, then, that the Church must be abolished, I mean that the exclusionary, comfortable Body of Christ, the body that has for so long refused the vocations of women, persecuted its prophets, neglected the truth, silenced its victims, protected its clergy and demonized lesbians, gays, bisexuals and trans people – must fall. And in the humility of that fall, and the simple nature of what would be left, it might baptize itself like the Saviour it proclaims and be renewed with the renewing waters it offers.

All too silent in the face of Black suffering is a Church that has unwittingly sold its soul – exchanging its eternal crown for the fading glory of the world. This church is one about whom many will conclude, largely from its silence and inaction against racism, that much of White Christianity considers itself either incapable of sin, freed from the necessity of repentance or exempt from the judgement of God. In other words, above the demands of the gospel. In relation to Black LGBTQ+ Christians whom the Church has forgotten to seek but not to accuse, portions of the Church will look back at this time as the moment when those seeking to follow Christ and serve him continued in a church that sold its birthright, abdicated its responsibility to God's children and abandoned the gospel it sought to proclaim. Actually, the suggestion that abolition is the answer to the Church's future is not that radical when in effect through its lack of inclusive love the Church has essentially, in the eyes of God, abolished itself.

When I call myself a Christian, I do so as one who has little affection for the mechanisms of the Church in its institutional embodiment. What I mean when I say that I am a Christian is that I am one who finds himself utterly compelled by the story, life, love, compassion, courage and care of Jesus Christ – that he makes sense to my life, my world and my reality. If those of us who are Black and LGBTQ+ are to find our home within Christ's story we must call out the places that claim to follow him yet exist as places where grace is in famine. We do not need to be pastors, preachers, priests or theologians – nor prophets, miracle-workers or long-time disciples … rather we need simply to be those who look at a crucified Jesus and take his wounds at their word. If he died for us, the Church is for us – it is ours too. If we are to have any future within and without the Church that does not exclude or discriminate against any of us, then we must return to the child in the manger at Bethlehem and commit, like God, to become small enough that others might be free. Ultimately, it is this that is the crux of the

Church's future – the question and task that lies ahead of the Christian community today is very simply this: can it become small like its Lord? If the Church is to be the extension of the incarnation into every corner of the world it must live as Jesus lives. It is, however, to each of us that the words of St Teresa of Avila are said:

> Christ has no body now but yours. No hands, no feet on earth but yours. Yours are the eyes through which he looks compassion on this world. Yours are the feet with which he walks to do good. Yours are the hands through which he blesses all the world. Yours are the hands, yours are the feet, yours are the eyes, you are his body. Christ has no body now on earth but yours.

The question for us who are Black and LGBTQ+ is: is this Jesus worth searching for? Is it possible, despite the failings of White Christianity and the homophobia of so many Black Churches, that this Jesus has something to offer that makes life more worth living? Can we allow the Church as it is to have the monopoly on God's grace? Can we allow that Jesus whom we know already to be our closest friend and greatest ally to be positioned as though he were against us when nothing of his earthly life says that it is so? If the Church is the place in which Jesus intended bread to be broken and wine to be poured out for *all* around one table and through one cup, he intended all his kin to live and worship in the intimacy of one family. Neither the Church nor we can be complete without attempting this.

We see now, that we have, in fact, come full circle. The questions asked in the Introduction by the blessed James Cone persist now, with even more force:

> When does the Church cease to be the Church of Jesus Christ? When do the Church's actions deny the faith that it verbalizes?

The Church ceases to be the Church of Jesus Christ in every place in which Black LGBTQ+ bodies are made unwelcome, are abused, demonized, unprotected and unloved. Wherever the Church silences our voices, denies the truth of our experience, or fails to publicly embrace and defend us – wherever our bodies become expendable – there too have Christ, his cross and his gospel. The Church's actions deny the faith it verbalizes every time it refuses to do what Jesus did, and love how Jesus loved. Every time we, as those who are LGBTQ+, engage with the tragicomic processes of the Church in which we are made to explain and defend our Christian and Queer existence, we are giving credibility to a church that has sold its birthright and lost its inheritance as Christ's body through its wilful hatred of us. There is nothing unconscious about the Church's bias towards the White, middle-class heterosexual, or those who aspire to fit within the broken church hierarchy that uses Jesus as the justification for its power. It is time to stop playing ball with the Church's injustice. Not by retreat, but by troublesome and prayerful presence.

Christ has made us, as we are, part of the Church, and the Church is ours, too. It must accept this, and live it, or it must be abolished. Standing as it does in denial of the gospel, it is a blasphemous testament to the all-inclusive love of the God it proclaims and the Christ it seeks to share with the world. Where it cannot love it must be called out, and where it does not welcome it must not be sustained. The Church has become for so many a place where the grace of God is in famine. It will not do, in this Church where even the soil is stultified, to open the windows and let in the fresh air. The lungs are diseased and the fruit of the soil rotten. What is needed is a conversion of the institutional will, and a transformation of the communal spirit, such that the heart of every Christian leader is convicted of the undeniable dignity and worth of every life, and every body, of every type, race, class and sexuality. It must submit itself to the truth about its life, and therefore it must submit to the Truth about all life, which is Jesus Christ.

Then, let the fruit of that repentance, born having faced the truth, be shown in a church that has at last loved us, desired us, Black and Queer, Holy and Beloved, just as Christ loves and desires us, and given its life for our lives, and made us a home in the only body capable of loving us all. The docility and infantilism that institutional Christianity induces must continually be resisted if those who have passed through the waters of baptism are to guard the fire which the Church, through its chosen method of being, seeks to control, if not totally extinguish. This fire is the fire that Christ ignited in the hearts of those he first called, and that is the inherited gift to all who follow Christ, or seek to follow and love him. It is this fire that is alight in the hearts of those the Church keeps outside its walls and safely away from its life-giving waters. Here, outside itself, in the neglected and oppressed, is its second Pentecost. Here, outside itself, is Christ its Lord. Locked out, knocking, wounded, alongside the Black Queer Beloved Children of God seeking the bread of life and cup of salvation ... and until it opens its doors, its heart, its mind and its ears, until it lengthens its tables and makes room in its sanctuaries, the Church must hear its own words, and bear them now to every area of its life:

Remember that you are dust, and to dust you shall return. Turn away from sin, and be faithful to Christ.[31]

Notes

1 Wendy Farley, *Gathering Those Driven Away: A Theology of Incarnation*, Louisville: Westminster John Knox Press, 2011, p. 3.

2 Leslie Weatherhead, *The Christian Agnostic*, London: Hodder & Stoughton, 1965.

3 Pope Paul VI, *Evangelii Nuntiandi*, 1975, ch. 1.15.

4 Karl Barth, *God Here and Now*, Oxford: Routledge, 2003, p. 39.

5 Ibid., pp. 42, 51.

6 Robert Thompson, in Julie Gittoes, Brutus Green and James Heard, *Generous Ecclesiology: Church, World and the Kingdom of God*, London: SCM Press, 2013, p. 146.

7 Thompson, in Gittoes et al., *Generous Ecclesiology*, p. 149.

8 www.youtube.com/watch?v=G4mWBKX_T8k, accessed 18.3.21.

9 A. D. A. France-Williams, *Ghost Ship*, London: SCM Press, 2020, p. 138.

10 James Baldwin, *Collected Essays: The Price of the Ticket*, New York: Library of America, 1998, p. 841.

11 James Baldwin, *Collected Essays: White Racism or World Community?* New York: Library of America, 1998, p. 752.

12 Ibid., p. 755

13 Ibid., p. 756.

14 France-Williams, *Ghost Ship*, p. 173.

15 Howard Thurman, *Jesus and the Disinherited*, Boston: Beacon Press, 1976, pp. 18–19.

16 Gittoes et al., *Generous Ecclesiology*, p. 102.

17 Kenneth Greet, *What Shall I Cry?* London: Epworth Press, 1986, p. 14.

18 Ibid., p. 94.

19 Fred Pratt Green, 'When Jesus came to Jordan', © 1980 Stainer & Bell Ltd.

20 George Burman Foster, *The Finality of the Christian Religion*, Chicago: University of Chicago Press, 1906, p. 187.

21 Benjamin E. Mays, *The Negro's God: As Reflected in His Literature*, Eugene: Wipf and Stock, 1938, p. 162.

22 Frances J. Crosby, 1891.

23 www.bbc.co.uk/news/uk-england-london-50815142, accessed 18.3.21.

24 www.huffingtonpost.co.uk/entry/spac-nation-investigated-over-financial-and-safeguarding-concerns_uk_5df38ffce4b04bcba1839541, accessed 18.3.21.

25 Anthony Reddie, *Theologizing Brexit: A Liberationist and Postcolonial Critique*, London: Routledge, 2020, p. 44.

26 bell hooks, *Rock My Soul: Black People and Self-Esteem*, New York: Washington Square Press, 2003, p. 223.

27 Reddie, *Theologizing Brexit*, p. 80.

28 M. Shawn Copeland. *Enfleshing Freedom: Body, Race, and Being*, Minneapolis: Fortress Press, 2010, p. 82.

29 Willie James Jennings, 'A Revolutionary Intimacy', sermon preached at Hope College, 2014, on Acts 11.1–3.

30 See www.youtube.com/watch?v=2i1XChVRwsY&t=1175s, accessed 7.4.21.

31 From 'The Liturgy of Ash Wednesday', *Common Worship: Times and Seasons*, London: Church House Publishing, 2012.

Epilogue

If Queerness is really about our shared experience of being made to feel different in the world, it seems to me that the Queer community can help the Church occupy the space it ought to occupy as a citizen of heaven in the midst of the world. The Vietnamese American writer Ocean Vuong said when reflecting on his identity:

> Being queer saved my life. Often we see queerness as deprivation. But when I look at my life, I saw that queerness demanded an alternative innovation from me. I had to make alternative routes; it made me curious; it made me ask, 'Is this enough for me?'[1]

The deep-searching nature of this question is one that I think is vital for Christians of the future – when looking at the Church as it is, we must ask: 'Is this enough?' We must dream bigger, not so much in relation to the Church in its essence – that is always the same – but the Church as it is embodied institutionally today: is this enough?

It has been the purpose of this book to break the Church's silence on Black LGBTQ+ lives in Britain, and to offer something gesturing towards an intersectional theology that centres and affirms Black British LGBTQ+ individuals and prioritizes our liberation in God's grace. I have been hesitant to label this work as a specialist theology, in part because I insist that 'Black British Queer theology' is mainstream, and that it is a failure of theologians, not of the Black British LGBTQ+ community, that we have been eluded for so long. I am aware, too, that the focus of this book has been Christian theology, and I hope that theologians and writers from a variety of faith traditions and none will engage with the Black British LGBTQ+

experience from a theological perspective. I believe that Black British LGBTQ+ people have a profound gift to offer theology and the Church – not least in terms of the work we have had to do in deconstructing the worst parts of a Christian heritage.

In many ways, writers and theologians who do not exist within the structures of the Church will find the ability to be more daring in their work when writing from a Black British LGBTQ+ perspective on sexuality and Christianity – not belonging as I and any priest does to the authoritarian system that institutional Christianity so often is. In a way, this too is part of the problem; that those who know the Church most intimately are unable so often to tell it the truth – we never have an honest critique of the systems that benefit us because such a critique is always an interrogation of the complicit self, and in this case a critique of the institution that houses and feeds us. Theologians who are members of the clergy are less likely to be entirely honest about their sexual experience too, which is deeply problematic. The most prophetic voices it seems to me will have to come from beyond the Church's systems of control and management, from those who are less invested in their own careers and relationships to the hierarchy, and who in the truest sense have nothing to lose. We need theologians who courageously continue to subvert narratives, betray boundaries, transgress expectations and answer honestly the question, 'Is this enough?'

Something clearly has to change. Pamela Lightsey challenges me deeply when she says that there is a need for us to

> queer those systems that are detrimental to the survival of an entire Black people. Like the young activist leaders, our goal is to disrupt, to deconstruct all that stands against the wellbeing of Black people.[2]

As Black LGBTQ+ people we must never assume that we belong where Whiteness has placed us, nor where heteronormativity, heteropatriarchy and the Christian Church would rather we did not venture. The queering of oppressive systems frees not just Black LGBTQ+ people, but all of us – this is why the ability to name (even when it is deeply uncomfortable) the explicit sites of privilege, racism, homophobia and transphobia is so much a fundamental part of the path towards justice and freedom. Once these sites are located, the Church, which is very good at clothing itself in the aesthetics of liberation, will need to do the work if it is to convince those it oppresses of its will to change.

There are fewer things of which I am more convinced than the fact that resisting easy answers to complex problems is essential in order to build the kind of future we need as a collective humanity. Part of the reason I am so restless in this world, and in this Church, is because the world we have isn't the world we're stuck with – it is the world we've settled for, the world we've made ... the world we don't seem to want to let go of. All these things are true of Christian community. It is a lie and a denial of reality to pretend as though this world 'works' for everyone, and a further lie to act as though the Church is one in which all people find welcome. The famine of grace is widespread and, like any unattended famine, will soon starve (and perhaps has begun to) even those who think that the famine is not their concern. A broken Church breaks us all, in the end. The Church in the United Kingdom faces a huge challenge if it is faithfully to proclaim the gospel to a society in which the message of the gospel, preached inclusively as it is, becomes increasingly hostile. Completing this book at a time when denial is perhaps the biggest threat to Church and society the biggest question I imagine most people have in their minds is: so what now? Where do we go from here?

When I spoke about the abolition of the Church, I was being serious. And many may wonder how it is that a person like me can talk about that with any sense of seriousness. As long as the righteous are convinced of a need to locate and condemn the sinful damned, the Church of Jesus Christ has a serious problem. Just at the point where as Christians we might find a common solidarity and fellowship in our sin, rather than our holiness, the LGBTQ+ individual becomes a scapegoat for all that others cannot face about their own lives. In such a Church, the marginalized and vulnerable will always be looted of their inherent dignity and worth. When I speak of abolition, I simply point towards the only way I can conceive of the Church actually surviving ... and what is important is the fact that the idea of abolition as a proposal is set against a Church that still has before it a choice: to repent and become what it must be to be the Church. Part of its repentance should look like clearer unequivocal statements on the inclusion of LGBTQ+ people within its life as a fundamental part of the gospel, the taking seriously of anti-racism work, long, hard and honest introspection on the state of its life, an interrogation of its power and, in the case of the Church of England, possible disestablishment. While so much of what has occurred in the history of the Church and its present leads me to think that repentance and the work towards repentance is impossible for the Church – as a preacher of the gospel, I remain a prisoner of hope. I know that the Holy Spirit can indeed convict and convert a broken society and even a fallen institution.

The power of the gospel is that at its heart exists a God who doesn't give up on anyone, who renews the very places thought to be barren, and who can turn a hopeless situation into an abundantly fruitful one. The Christian God is a God who is powerful only in powerlessness, made tangible by Christ's vulnerable humanity, and known only through an all-encompassing love. This means that even those of us who think our diagnosis of a situation is accurate must be wary of telling God where God can and cannot work. There is always the danger of becoming just as ignorant and little minded as Christians who are conservative and subscribe to an exclusionary Christianity. The challenge of the gospel is that it means that easy answers will never work – that anything short of love and the fullness of love in response to the societal challenges we face as human beings will never do. As tempting as it can be to think of a church where we are surrounded by those who are just like us, such a church will still fail to truly be the Church. And so all utopias must in the end be avoided, primarily because 'All paradises, all utopias are designed by who is not there, by the people who are not allowed in',[3] and are therefore still exclusionary. If my idea of heaven, or my idea of the Church of the future, is one void of White people or heterosexual Christians then both White people and heterosexuals have shaped even my idea of eternity, my vision of the future ...

such a limitation on my imagination of eternity is still oppression. Our speech, our churches and our imaginations must in every sense become much more capacious as we excavate the depths of what it means to be human and unafraid. It is in that spaciousness that we can confront not only personal sin but structural sin, in that space when we can rediscover the narrative of grace for those for whom such a narrative has disappeared, and in that space that the Church can do its work of repentance and reparation.

The hope, if there is any, is that the gospel provides us with both the challenge and the solution – that if there is grace for the Black LGBTQ+ Christian, there is grace too for the Church. Where in a broken world the language of politics tells us to say, 'What if that was your brother, your son, your sister, your friend, your father?', the language of the gospel tells us, 'That is your brother, your sister, your daughter, your son, your father, your sibling, your friend, your kin – you ... the image and likeness of God.' The Christian faith has something profound to say about God's action in the world, and the only hope of social renewal is a renewal of hearts that find their common centre in the heart of the totally other, and thereby in the heart of God. Until we radically love our neighbour with the love that they are due in Christ, until we know deeply ourselves to be loved, we are the wilful architects of our own demise. The catch is, that in this task of restoration and renewal, of repentance and reparation, of truth-telling and truth-hearing, it is the Church who, like God in sending us Jesus Christ, now needs to make the first move. And we, who have been hurt by the Body of Christ, will come to trust it only by its posture toward us.

Notes

1 Ocean Vuong, https://podcasts.apple.com/us/podcast/all-the-ways-to-be-with-bryan-washington-ocean-vuong/id1351044991?i=100050 3092145, accessed 18.3.21.

2 Pamela Lightsey, *Our Lives Matter*, Oregon: Wipf and Stock, 2015, p. 98.

3 Toni Morrison, www.pbs.org/newshour/show/toni-morrison, accessed 18.3.21.

Appendix
Sustaining Grace: Seated at the Right Hand of Zaddy

The glory of God is a human being fully alive; and the life of a human being consists in their beholding God.

Irenaeus of Lyon[1]

Calling God 'Zaddy' is a subversive move towards deconstructing some of the language we inherit around how we address God. It might not seem respectful, or appropriate, but what real relationship of intimacy ever exists consistently within those boundaries and barriers? Part of what it means to be a free human being with a spiritual centre is the freedom to explore what spirituality means to us as those who are Black and LGBTQ+. When I asked friends who have left the Church, but who are Black and LGBTQ+, what they thought a book like this could do, and what would be a key component of this book, they all said in different ways:

'Teach us to pray!'

Of course, prayer is a lifelong practice of intercourse with God, and I'm still finding my way, but this didn't entirely surprise me. I know that many of us who exist beyond the walls of our faith communities do not always occupy that space of exile by choice, but by circumstance. Within us there is a longing for the spiritual, a yearning to connect with the Divine, and as Christians a deep desire to offer to God in Jesus Christ our praise and our prayer. We who are Black and LGBTQ+ are courageous every day in a world that does not want us to see tomorrow. As Black LGBTQ+ people our bodies (maybe too our souls?) are themselves sites of resistance, weapons of activism. We are always fighting for air, for room, for freedom. Grace, in the life of the one who sees themselves as God sees them, must be sustained not just grasped. Sustained through intimacy with the One who says anew to us each day:

'You are mine ...
... and you are Black and beautiful!'

If it is true that love enables us to take off our masks, then prayer and meditation, as the place in which we nurture our love for God and God's love for us, is the space in which we stand in our Black Queer nakedness before God. When God comes close to us, we see that Jesus isn't restricted to the Whiteness of stained-glass windows, but is always willing to chill in our presence and have us chill with him as one who is Black and Queer. Jesus is the one who meets us in reggae and afrobeats, in gospel and bashment, in the breaking of hard dough bread and the drinking of Sorrell, the pounding of yam and the grilling of fish. He is, if truly God as I believe, the Jesus of egusi, bami, snapper and Jollof. Jesus has given us Fela and Jill Scott, Burna Boy and Noname Gypsy, Bob Marley and Oumou Sangaré – everything that seeks to force us to divorce our world in its totality from our Ancient God is not of God. The revolutionary intimacy we so desperately need in the world begins perhaps with our drawing near to God and letting God draw near to us. The prayers that follow are just an attempt at offering something that might enable short and simple prayers – use/write your own if you feel so led. People might find it useful to burn some incense, use a singing bowl, place an icon of Jesus or one of the saints, or light a candle somewhere special in a space in which to pray ... what's most important is that we nurture spaces and practices that allow ourselves to feel at home as we are, in the presence of the God who made us and loves us. This is put so perfectly in words from the prophet Isaiah:

But now thus says the Lord,
   he who created you, O Jacob,
   he who formed you, O Israel:
Do not fear, for I have redeemed you;
   I have called you by name, you are mine.
When you pass through the waters, I will be with you;
   and through the rivers, they shall not overwhelm you;
when you walk through fire you shall not be burned,
   and the flame shall not consume you.
For I am the Lord your God,
   the Holy One of Israel, your Saviour.
I give Egypt as your ransom,
   Ethiopia and Seba in exchange for you.
Because you are precious in my sight,
   and honoured, and I love you,

Isaiah 43.1–4

A Prayer for Each Day

Lord, Help me to see you
as you are.

Myself as you
see me.

Others as I
should see them.

Until I see you
face to face.
Amen.

A Prayer for Each Night

Loving God,
As this day began with you,
So too does this day end with you.
You have been with me in every moment,
And I ask that here, at the end of this day,
You would continue to be with me –
Where I have sinned, I ask forgiveness,
Where I have been sinned against, help me to forgive –
May I forgive myself as you forgive me.
Hide me under the shadow of your wing,
Keep me as the apple of your eye –
You are my resting place, my refuge –
My sweet protection and my God.
So as I sleep, may I sleep in your love,
And as I rise, may I rise renewed – to face the tomorrow
   that is already in your hands.
Amen.

A Prayer of Confession

Jesus, It's me.
I've messed up,
I ... *(tell God whatever is on your heart to confess)*

Hold me in your love,
Comfort me in your grace,
Assure me of your mercy.

In you, I am cherished,
known, forgiven,
and set free.

Amen.

A Prayer of Intercession

God of the poor and weak,
God of the vulnerable and marginalized,
I place *(name situation/person/place)*
In your hands – may your Holy Spirit
Work the beauty of your power in *(insert name)*
That your life, health and peace,
Which passes all understanding –
Might be made known.
Amen.

A Meditation for Those Who Do Not Feel Loved

There is ...
No part of me that God despises
No part of me God has not made
No part of me God does not love
No part of me God has not redeemed
Nothing about me God does not know
Nothing in my appearance God does not like
Nothing that can make God love me more
Nothing that can make God love me less
No burden God will not help me carry
No comfort he does not want me to know
No joy he wants me to deny
No trial he will abandon me in
No God worth knowing who is not Love.

A Prayer to Our Lady of Abolition

Hail Mary,
full of grace and courage,
destroyer of babylon,
defender against White Supremacy, injustice, hatred ...
pray for us who suffer under the powers of algorithms,
presidencies and parliaments ... we who suffer under the
inequalities and legacies of Empire and its chokehold – we
who cause the suffering to suffer and who look upon the
darknesses we know, but cannot name.
May the Lord be with us, O Holy, Black, Mother of God,
as he is with you.
May you lead us, insurgents maladjusted to the world, to
the dazzling Blackness of your Son.
And, until the proud are scattered in the delusions of their
hearts and the fearful surrounded by mercy.
Until the mighty are brought down, and the lowly lifted up.
Until the hungry are filled and the rich sent away empty.
Until then ...
Pray for us, Mother of Ferguson, Mother of Minneapolis,
Mother of Palestine, Mother of Yemen, Mother of
Beirut, Mother of all who cannot, but yearn with you, to
breathe ...

Note

1 Irenaeus, *Against Heresies*, Book 4, chapter 34, section 7.

Index of Names and Subjects

Lightning Source UK Ltd.
Milton Keynes UK
UKHW010808181022
410662UK00004B/157